SOVIET INTERNMENT

SOVIET INTERNMENT

MEMORY, NOSTALGIA, AND THE POW EXPERIENCE

Maria Cristina Galmarini

BLOOMSBURY ACADEMIC

LONDON • NEW YORK • OXFORD • NEW DELHI • SYDNEY

BLOOMSBURY ACADEMIC
Bloomsbury Publishing Plc, 50 Bedford Square, London, WC1B 3DP, UK
Bloomsbury Publishing Inc, 1359 Broadway, New York, NY 10018, USA
Bloomsbury Publishing Ireland, 29 Earlsfort Terrace, Dublin 2, D02 AY28, Ireland

BLOOMSBURY, BLOOMSBURY ACADEMIC and the Diana logo are
trademarks of Bloomsbury Publishing Plc

First published in Great Britain 2025

Series design by Tjaša Krivec
Cover image: World War 2, 57,600 German soldiers, taken prisoner in the
last few days by the troops of the 1st, 2nd, and 3rd Belorussian fronts,
being marched through the streets of Moscow on their way to
POW camps, July 17, 1944 © Sovfoto / Getty Images

A catalogue record for this book is available from the British Library.

A catalog record for this book is available from the Library of Congress.

ISBN: HB: 978-1-3505-0773-9
          PB: 978-1-3505-0774-6
          ePDF: 978-1-3505-0775-3
          eBook: 978-1-3505-0776-0

Series: Russian Shorts

Typeset by Integra Software Services Pvt. Ltd.
Printed and bound in Great Britain

For product safety related questions contact productsafety@bloomsbury.com.

To find out more about our authors and books visit www.bloomsbury.com
and sign up for our newsletters.

To Flavia, in loving memory

CONTENTS

FIGURES

All figures are reprinted courtesy of Olga Avdiukova.

PROLOGUE

The march toward the camps was mercilessly mowing down the long columns of prisoners. As Umberto Montini walked, stumbling over corpses and propelled by the angry shouts of his Soviet captors, he vowed that, if he had survived the ordeal, he would have never celebrated that day anymore. It was Christmas, December 25, 1942, and the Italian Army in Russia (ARMIR) had just been defeated by the Soviet Union's Red Army. While many of his fellow soldiers died on the way or soon after reaching the POWs' labor camps, Umberto had the good fortune to be barreled to the Zubova Poliana prisoners' hospital in the Autonomous Soviet Socialist Republic of Mordovia, approximately 500 kilometers South-East of Moscow. There, thanks to the care and affection that doctor Polina Evteevna Ovodkova provided him, he not only recovered his physical health but also learned to tolerate his "depression." Polina's "comfort"—as Umberto called the special attention she gave him—sustained the Italian captive through his three years of imprisonment.[1] Its memory refused to subside in him even upon his repatriation to Italy in the fall of 1945. To the contrary, growing stronger with the passing of time and his disappointment in Italian politics, the memory of both the doctor Polina and the hospital Zubova Poliana generated in him a complicated sense of nostalgia for the Soviet world he had left behind.

---

[1]Unless otherwise indicated, all words in quotation marks are direct quotes from either Umberto Montini's (UM) or Anfisa Serzhanina's (AS) private archives. To reduce the number of footnotes and because the same words often reappear verbatim in different memory installments and letters, I put all citations in one footnote per paragraph. In this case, UM, Umberto to Sandra Bortolin, 12.4.1993; Commenti, 30.7.1993 and 28.3.1994.

Soviet Internment

In this book, I reconstruct Umberto's experience and memory of war and internment through an analysis of his copious writings, including his personal notes and the letters he exchanged with a former hospital worker fifty years after his repatriation. My aim is to investigate the testimony of a surviving Second World War prisoner, whose memories were haunted by the fury of war and whose body carried deep physical and emotional traces but who nonetheless felt a nostalgic attachment to his place of internment. At the center of my attention is a memorial narrative that, while preserving some fundamental features of the soldiers' and prisoners' memoirs genre, is also quite unique within it. Not only did Umberto experience the Soviet front as a non-fighting soldier (he served as his unit's German language interpreter) and was interned in a hospital instead of a labor camp, but he also refused to "demonize" the Soviet state and its people. Umberto admired several aspects of the communist socio-political order as he had known it in the microcosm of Zubova Poliana and felt a "debt of gratitude to Russia and the Russians"—as he indiscriminately referred to the local citizens whether they were Russians or from one of the many other nationalities making up the Soviet Union. He thought "the Russians" had "saved [his] life" and "helped him be born again" after he had metaphorically died in the war.[2] In short, this former POW believed he had a counternarrative to tell, one in which prisoners do not appear as victims of the Soviet state and in which veterans' anger should be targeted at fascist propaganda, the inefficiency of the Italian Army in the Second World War, and the injustice of the Italian postwar welfare system.

Umberto's remarkably rich personal archive found its way to me in 2022. It was a gift from fellow historian and old friend Giorgio Scotoni (who in turn had received it from Umberto in the mid-1990s) and presented itself as a private archive containing forty-eight pages of Umberto's recollections, thirty-five letters from hospital worker Anfisa Serzhanina, and Umberto's comments to twenty-one of them. Encountering these materials at a time when the Russian Federation's full-scale invasion of Ukraine had just begun devastating areas not

---

[2] AS, Umberto to Anfisa, 20.9.1993.

too far away from those where Umberto had been captured in 1942, I was immediately captivated by this man's testimonial discourse. However, the temptation to turn Umberto's archival traces into a book became truly impossible to ignore for me around one year later, when Anfisa Serzhanina's archive came to me, too. Another dear colleague and friend, historian Maria Romashova, had been able to track down Anfisa's surviving relatives in Perm' and, after some hard digging, had discovered that Anfisa had preserved sixty-eight of the ninety letters Umberto wrote to her between 1993 and 1999. These epistles were at times quite difficult to decipher because Umberto had written them in his own hand in Russian (although using an awkward mix of Russian words and Italian syntax). Many of them were still in their original envelopes, which often included also clippings from Italian newspapers, postcards from Bolzano, and photographs of the Montini family.[3] Together with his autobiographical installments in Italian and Anfisa's letters in Russian that were preserved in Umberto's private archive, these multilingual sources made his story visible to me in unique ways.

Indeed, although opaque and incomplete in some aspects, the two family archives not only helped me see the outline of former soldier Montini's life quite clearly, from his birth in 1922 to his death in 2003, but also gave me the possibility to reflect on the complex memory journey that he undertook in the last ten years of his existence. Furthermore, offering observations on events across nearly eighty years of European history, Umberto's and Anfisa's recollections and letters invited me to rethink my own historical memory as a European person. Umberto commented on historical figures such as Benito Mussolini and Josef Stalin; he gave evocative and controversial portraits of the militarization of Italian youth under Fascism, the culture of the Soviet camps during the Second World War, and the fallacies of democracy

---

[3]Umberto's son, Aldo Montini, gave me permission to use his father's writings, while Anfisa's granddaughter, Olga Avdiukova, has authorized me to analyze and quote from her grandmother's materials. Additional archival traces about Umberto are preserved in an uncatalogued archival collection named after him in the Italian Historical Museum of War in Rovereto and in the Historical Archive of the City of Bolzano. I am grateful to archivists Nicola Fontana and Patrizia Fedeli for facilitating my access to them.

in postwar Italy, whilst also discussing the Cold War, the nature of the Soviet system, the reasons why Mikhail Gorbachev's reform program of "perestroika" failed, and the state of the world after the collapse of the USSR. Finally, because his scattered and fragmented recollections often served as springboards for his efforts to heal from lingering war trauma, they also raised in me urgent questions on the relationship between testimonial discourse, mental health, and political ideology. How can surviving soldiers and prisoners testify to an experience whose memory remains a gaping wound? Is narration able to heal trauma and erase the horrors witnessed during the war? And how does trauma affect the creation of alternative politics of memory?

These questions are the red threads running through the book's chapters. I begin to address them in Chapter 1 by discussing the circumstances in which our protagonist undertook his journey of public remembrance, his motivations for doing so, the difficulties he encountered, and the individuals who accompanied him on it. This genealogy of Umberto's memory and narration provides references to some of the historiographical and theoretical approaches that have informed my thinking as I strove to make sense of Umberto's archive and the way he wanted his story to be known. It also offers a framework to read critically the chronological exposition of Umberto's life that follows in the remaining chapters. There, I focus on four key moments: his fascist youth and the call to arms, the "Russian front," his internment at Zubova Poliana, and his repatriation and readaptation to postwar Italy. By reconstructing these phases of Umberto's biography, in Chapters 2 through 5 my goal is to evoke not only his thoughts but above all his emotions through the details that remained impressed his memory. To achieve this goal, I replicate the aesthetics mobilized by Umberto in the staging of his war experience. This means that, in my own exposition of his story, I strive to respect his narratological choices, preserve the images he decided to conjure, and recreate his inner world and most salient affects. The outcome is an account that brings back to life the episodes that punctuated Umberto's life as he remembers them, regardless of whether they are true or not. To make it clear, I am not concerned with the accuracy and reliability of Umberto's testimony as a source of documentary knowledge about the past. Rather, following the eminent historian Dominick LaCapra's influential work, I see his testimony as a source that "bring[s] theoretical concerns in sustained contact with [individuals'] experience[s]."[4]

In Umberto's case, crucial among these "theoretical"—and historiographical—"concerns" (besides the role of memory in coming to terms with a traumatic past) are the issues of political development in ordinary twentieth-century Europeans, the ideological consequences of the Second World War, and the supposed triumph of democratic values at the end of the Cold War. In the 1930s, the fascist regime had attempted to transform the Italian people into New Fascist Men and Women, thereby striving to create for itself a necessary foundation of popular consensus. Like many other of his contemporaries, Umberto was involved in several of the party's associations and saw himself as a good fascist man. During the war, however, he was obliged to recognize the demise of the political movement that he had formerly supported. In addition, after encountering fascist propaganda in his adolescence, at Zubova, Umberto experienced Soviet political indoctrination. Thanks to a program of what the Stalinist state called "political re-education," in the POW hospital he began to appreciate the virtues of Soviet communism and, in fact, preserved communist sympathies throughout his life. Thus, in December 1995, he rejoiced at Gennady Zyuganov's Communist Party victory in the Russian Duma elections, believing that, albeit with some "modernization and reform," the communist "orientation" was the right one for Russia. Conversely, writing in the wake of the "*mani pulite*" (clean hands) corruption scandals and the rise of Silvio Berlusconi's party Forza Italia, Umberto complained about the rise of the right in Italian politics.[5]

"Conversion" from Fascism to Communism marked the experience of other POWs, too. For instance, historian Maria Teresa Giusti has examined the story of Danilo Ferretti, whose Soviet diary tells of his

---

[4]Dominick LaCapra, *Writing History, Writing Trauma* (Baltimore, MD: John Hopkins University Press, 2001), xiv.
[5]AS, Umberto to Anfisa, 22.12.1995.

"inner evolution" and transformation into a "model communist."[6] Similarly, an historical study by Sherzod Muminov has found that, in a few Japanese POWs, Marxist ideology replaced the imperial doctrine that they had followed before internment.[7] Umberto, however, never turned into an exemplary communist. Although he lamented the presence of neo-fascist feelings among the Italian youth, he himself often repeated fascist discourses about the instability and unpredictability of democratic parliamentarism and continued to nurture fascist approaches to gender and race. For instance, he believed that women should not be employed in the national labor force but work only in the home. As he was concerned, the desire of contemporary Italian couples to have two salaries coming in each month was triggered by fantasies of richness ("so they can buy a fur coat"), but it was the children who paid the price as they were not raised by their mothers. In even less acceptable terms, Umberto lamented the presence of "many negros and people from Africa," who "do not work" and live off criminality and the Italian state's welfare.[8] Finally—and most paradoxically—besides the ideal of equality and justice, the virtues that 70-year-old Umberto so strongly appreciated in Soviet communism were exactly those features of order, discipline, and obedience that he had internalized as a young man in fascist Italy.

How successful then were first fascist and later communist "conversion" efforts in the longer run? Judging from Umberto's writings, it appears that the extent to which he distanced himself from Fascism and became Sovietized (in terms of ideological content) is rather questionable. The war had certainly been a rupture in his political views, but, despite his emphasis on ideological transformation, Umberto did not completely break with earlier beliefs, attitudes, and mental dispositions. Especially his sense of what

---

[6]Maria Teresa Giusti, "Dal fascismo al communism: il diario di prigionia di Danilo Ferretti," in *"La propaganda e' l'unica nostra cultura." Scritture autobiografiche dal fronte sovietico (1941–1943)*, ed. Quinto Antonelli (Trento: Fondazione Museo Storico Trentino, 2016), 125–57.

[7]Sherzod Muminov, *Eleven Winters of Discontent: The Siberian Internment and the Making of a New Japan* (Cambridge, MA: Harvard University Press, 2022).

[8]AS, Umberto to Anfisa, 28.9.1995 and 5.2.1996.

constituted legitimate government seemed not to have fundamentally changed. He just became increasingly wary of politics and developed a pragmatic attitude: he craved "order" and "another Stalin," and was more concerned with obtaining what he needed (recognition of war invalid status and its related welfare benefits) than challenging political authority through democratic participation. Indeed, unlike Danilo Ferretti, Umberto never joined the Italian Communist Party, and his nostalgia for the Soviet era was rooted not so much in coherent Marxist political convictions but rather in the human connections he had developed during his internment. Whether or not we ultimately interpret this twenty-century man as an "authoritarian personality,"[9] what remains indisputable is his conviction that all politics is "dirty," something that "destroys peace," "starts wars," and "brings damage" to ordinary people.[10] Striving to make sense of his discourses of suffering, bereavement, and loss as well as love and longing we are not only forced to confront the legacies of a common European traumatic past but also to reflect on how personal experiences of military conflict and displacement to this day continue to affect ordinary Europeans' political trajectories and loyalties.

---

[9]Theodor Adorno, Else Frenkel-Brenswik, Daniel J. Levinson and R. Nevitt Sanford, *The Authoritarian Personality* (New York: Verso Books, 2019).
[10]AS, Umberto to Anfisa, 3.5.1995, 20.9.1993, and 29.6.1994.

CHAPTER 1
A GENEALOGY OF MEMORY AND NARRATION

The year 1992 marked the fiftieth anniversary of the Italian Army's (ARMIR) defeat on the Don River. It was also the year when a new country, the Russian Federation, was born from the ashes of the recently collapsed Soviet Union. Both events created a media frenzy and, as Italian public culture was saturated with newspaper articles, books, and television programs about Russia, Umberto Montini felt the need to add his witness voice to them. On the one hand, he was angry at how Italian journalists and "self-proclaimed" writers were "falsifying" and "domesticating" the story of the ARMIR, passing their "fictions" about it for "history." It was a "lie," he insisted, that the ARMIR was a "lost army."[1] Rather, the army had been "sacrificed, abandoned, and perhaps even … sold." Umberto believed that only he knew this uncomfortable "truth," a "truth" that the Italian state "forbid to reveal" despite its loud proclamations of "freedom" and "democracy," and a "truth" that "many did not want to hear." On the other hand, as instances of the former Soviet Union's backwardness and brutality made headlines, Umberto was livid at the biases of the agents of Italian public culture and eager to "fight" their "disinformation" campaign. Feeling that he had a "debt of gratitude" toward "Russia and the Russians," which—he claimed—was unrelated to any party belonging or political leaning, he sought to pay it by making his personal story publicly known and thereby shape Italians' collective memory of the recently collapsed USSR in more positive ways.[2]

---

[1] Pino Scaccia, *ARMIR: Sulle Tracce di un Esercito Perduto* (Torino: Nuova ERI, 1992).
[2] UM, "Precisazioni"; "Reminescenze." AS, Umberto to Anfisa 20.9.1993 and 21.1.1997.

Journalists were not the only source of Umberto's chagrin. He was also resentful and disappointed at how other survivors were allegedly bearing witness. Among them, for instance, was Eugenio Corti, a former officer of the same 30th Army Corps Artillery Grouping in which Umberto had served. Having miraculously come back alive from the Eastern front, Corti had published several accounts about it. Umberto, however, believed that Corti had "ignobly exploited [the defeat] to indulge his fantasy." His books, in Umberto's view, provided the readers only with "few true facts and circumstances," making up and fictionalizing much of the rest so as to sell better. The diary that this survivor claimed to have kept during the retreat was a fake, as Umberto was concerned.[3] Corti's grouping had endured the first hit of the heavy Soviet blow; it had been dispersed by it; and the few who had survived it had retreated in a completely disorderly manner. In Umberto's opinion, it would have been "impossible" for anybody to write "a real diary" chronicling "those terrible days." As he argued: "Anybody who attempts to chronicle that sudden—although predictable—disarray is obliged to falsify the truth; he is forced to relive nightmares in his mind, which in some cases might be close to reality," but cannot be presumed to be true.[4]

Furthermore, as Italian state authorities in the wake of Gorbachev's opening to the West attempted to find the remains of Second World War casualties in the Soviet Union, this act of reckoning with the dead pushed Umberto to rethink his past too. Already in 1984, the former Alpini corps officer and Second World War veteran Guido Vettorazzo undertook a research trip to the Don, followed by six more journeys along the routes of the war, all aimed at visiting former detention sites and identifying possible mass graves.[5] A few years later, in April 1991, the Italian Ministry of Defense's *Onor Caduti* (Commissariat

---

[3]Here Umberto referred to Corti's *I più non ritornano. Diario di ventotto giorni d'accerchiamento russo, nell'inverno 1942–43* originally published in 1947 by Garzanti and then re-published in 1993 by Mursia.

[4]UM, "Reminescenze."

[5]Guido Vettorazzo, *Cento Lettera dalla Russia 1942–1943* (Rovereto: Museo Storico Italiano della Guerra, 1993).

Honoring the Fallen of War) signed a bilateral agreement with the Soviet Union "on the state of burial grounds."[6] As part of it, the Soviet authorities delivered to their Italian counterparts their so-far secreted listings of military personnel captured by the Red Army during the war. Covering over 400 camps and listing around 64,400 names, these records made it possible to pinpoint the place of internment and the date of death of thousands of men previously labeled as missing in action. In addition, this Italo-Soviet agreement also allowed the Italian government to send a special expedition to the Soviet Union. Led by General Benito Gavazza and including volunteers from the Italian National Union of Veterans of Russia (*Unione Nazionale Italiana Reduci di Russia*, or UNIRR), this expedition was only able to perform a few exhumations because the remains were hardly recognizable after so many years in mass graves. Still, it placed tombstones and commemorative signs in all the identified burial areas, including prisoners' camps and hospitals in the regions of Ekaterinburg, Nizhnyi Novgorod, Tambov, and Vladimir as well as in the Autonomous Republic of Mordovia.[7]

Umberto eagerly read all public reports about Vettorazzo's research trips and Gavazza's expedition. As soon as the *Onor Caduti* published the lists it received from the Soviet Union, he rushed to purchase copies of them.[8] What he read, however, further angered him. Not only did the Italian government and the UNIRR's publications exaggerate the number of Italian POWs who had died in Soviet internment by setting it at around 60,000, but, even more annoyingly to him, they presented

---

[6] The agreement was later ratified by the Russian Federation. See "Accordo tra Italia e Federazione Russa sullo status dei luoghi di sepoltura dei militari italiani in Russia e dei militari russi in Italia caduti nella II guerra mondiale," *Gazzetta Ufficiale della Repubblica Italiana*. Serie Generale n. 164 del 15-07-1996, Suppl. Ordinario n. 119, 9–12.

[7] Ministero della Difesa, *CSIR-ARMIR. Campi di prigionia e fosse comuni* (Gaeta: Stabilimento Grafico Militare, 1996); and Carlo Vicentini, *Rapporto sui prigionieri di guerra italiani in Russia* (Roma: UNIRR, 1995).

[8] Commissariato generale onoranze caduti in guerra, *Elenco ufficiale dei prigionieri italiani deceduti nei lager russi: traslitterati dai tabulati dell'Archivio storico dell'ex U.R.S.S.: documentazione ufficiale del Ministero della difesa, Commissariato generale per le onoranze ai caduti in Guerra*, 5 volumes (Milano: UNIRR, 1993).

as a new discovery something that he had always known. Namely, the location of unmarked graves at Zubova.[9]

Thus, that year of commemoration and change enabled Italian public opinion to have a new vantage point on both the war and the former Soviet Union. As for Umberto, the imperative to set the historical record straight and the perception of drastic discontinuity authorized him to embark on a journey of public re-evocation and active witnessing. This chapter reveals that this journey was a deliberate memory work that took Umberto in many unforeseen directions and forced him to penetrate a dark universe which, for many years, he had attempted to erase.

A Testimony Both Usual and Unusual

Umberto's first attempt at bringing his testimony into the public sphere took the form of two television appearances, neither of which ultimately satisfied his desire to be heard. First, he gave an interview to Sandra Bortolin, a journalist working for the Bolzano branch of the television channel RAI TRE, on December 24, 1992, the very anniversary of his capture.[10] Then, on February 22, 1993, he appeared on RAI UNO's program "Caffe' Italiano," where he was interviewed by the well-known journalist Elisabetta Gardini. On both occasions, Umberto remembered doctor Polina Ovodkova and claimed that he had overcome all diseases and epidemics only thanks to the care he had received from "the Russians." Both times, however, he was disappointed at the way the interviewing journalist treated him. As it seemed to him, nobody wanted "the truth" about the war to be told. Especially regarding the program "Caffe' Italiano," he believed that its producers had "shamelessly" used him to raise the show's poor ratings: they had advertised that he would reveal new information about the ARMIR but then prevented him from

---

[9]AS, Umberto to Anfisa 10.4.1996.
[10]Centro di archiviazione RAI BOLZANO, teca T92359/051, programma "Regione Sette," servizio "Reduce Armir," 24.12.1992.

saying what he really wanted to say. Denying him the opportunity to uncover "uncomfortable and controversial facts," Gardini had only allowed him to tell an episode concerning the death of a fellow soldier. As regards Polina, the story of how she saved his life had been deprived of its potential to show the Soviet people's compassion and just reduced to a case of good luck. "Obviously," he concluded after this interview, "no so-called democratic freedom" truly existed in Italy.[11]

Although certainly frustrating, these television appearances were nonetheless constructive moments in Umberto's memory journey. Preparing for their interviews with him, RAI UNO journalists had searched for Polina and discovered what had happened to her. As the TV channel's correspondent in Moscow, Demetrio Volcic told Umberto live during the program, right after the war Polina had married a military doctor named Andrei Beliaev. Together, they had first lived in Siberia; then, in 1956, they had moved to East Germany; and later, in 1963, they had settled in Leningrad, where they had raised their two sons Vladimir and Evgenii, and where Polina had prematurely passed away in 1978 at the age of sixty. This news not only provided Umberto with some closure but also motivated him even more to spread the "truth" on how the doctor Polina had nursed him back to health at the hospital of Zubova Poliana.

In addition, despite all the disappointment it caused him, appearing on national television gave the former POW Montini significant visibility. Some journalists picked up his story and disseminated his "truth" through the pages of both local and national newspapers.[12] Even more importantly, after the RAI UNO show, Umberto began to receive an increasing number of telephone calls from former fellow prisoners. They, too, had not been able to forget the war and, burdened with the ballast of the past, suffered from the same pain that Umberto

---

[11]UM, Commenti 30.1.1994; and AS, Umberto to Anfisa 20.9.1993.

[12]Giuseppe Ferrandi, "La', in Russia. L'odissea terribile di un prigioniero di guerra," *Alto Adige*, March 1, 1993; Giuseppe Ferrandi, "Diro' la verita'. La rabbia di Umberto Montini reduce di Russia," *Alto Adige*, March 7, 1993; and w.ca., "Ero in Russia con due vercellesi e so dove sono stati sepolti," *La Stampa*, July 15, 1993.

felt. At the same time, for them like for Umberto, the unforgettability of the war did not necessarily translate in the capacity to remember it clearly, let alone describe it factually. They were all trapped in the nightmares and horrors of fractured images ("photograms" as Umberto called them) that were deeply impressed in their minds, but they were incapable of producing a straightforward, controlled, and orderly chronological narrative of what had happened to them at the front. While Umberto shared this condition with fellow former POWs, the exchange of emotional memories with them also fortified his mnemonic process: he felt that, albeit still erratic, his memory was becoming neater and his capacity for narration greater. With each telephone call and later through mutual visits, a growing number of forgotten details were coming back to life for him as though he had "lived through them just yesterday." As Umberto wrote in a note to himself, when he and his comrades reminisced about Zubova's nurses, guards, and political commissars, these individuals became "characters" and started to function as "lighthouses dissipating the fog [of time]."[13]

These statements on how conversations with other POWs revealed to Umberto the content of previously hidden memories must be taken critically. Certainly, they helped him create a "community of remembrance"—as historian of German veterans' collective memory Christiane Wienand has called this phenomenon—and offered him a way to access and evaluate his memories and experiences.[14] Yet, as the American psychologist Jerome Bruner has argued, "any autobiographical reconfiguring of a life … is not so much a matter of making new discoveries in the archeological record of our experience … but of rewriting a narrative along different interpretative lines."[15] Previously irrelevant facts became relevant to Umberto precisely during his conversations with other former captives. And it was the

---

[13]UM, "Sorvolando" and Commenti, 30.10.1993.

[14]Christiane Wienand, *Returning Memories: Former Prisoners of War in Divided and Reunited Germany* (Rochester, NY: Camden House, 2015).

[15]Jerome Bruner, "The Autobiographical Process," in *The Culture of Autobiography. Constructions of Self-Representation*, ed. Robert Folkenflik (Stanford: Stanford University Press, 1993), 38–56, at 40.

new salience of certain memories that now pushed him to engage in something completely new: the writing of his memoirs.

The elderly veteran established a writing routine for himself, a sort of protocol that he systematically followed: each morning, after he woke up from a restless sleep and before "depression" progressively overcame him during the day, he sat in his office—which he fittingly called "my Russian museum"—and typed out his recollections, every day adding some new autobiographical installments to his archive.[16] The sustained effort to record all memories in writing was not painless for him (and not only because it pushed him to relieve his traumas). Umberto had only finished middle school and was unused to writing; he did not feel confident about his clarity of exposition and his capacity to string episodes into a plot; he knew that his text would contain multiple mistakes; and he feared that it might also be filled with repetitions and overwhelming details (as indeed it is). But the outcome—Umberto hoped—would be a book that differed from all other survivors' accounts and that was uniquely capable of delivering the "truth."

In fact, the testimony Umberto ultimately produced is simultaneously usual and unusual, in many respects representative of a certain genre (which scholar Samuel Hynes has called "the soldiers' tale"), while also diverging from it in others.[17] Governing the literary conventions in which autobiographical accounts of war and/or internment are written, this genre demands that the author trace a trajectory of descent into hell to show how such an experience was lived before being overcome. For Umberto, specifically, hell started out when the Italian Army Command issued a retreat order and the ARMIR's soldiers began to walk in the cold steppe desperately trying to break out of Soviet encirclement. Then, hell became progressively more unbearable as Umberto was captured by the Red Army, forced on a seven-day march by foot, and finally loaded on a cargo train and taken to his place of internment. Umberto's prose

---

[16]UM, Umberto to Bortolin, 12.4.1993.
[17]Samuel Hynes, *The Soldiers' Tale: Bearing Witness to Modern War* (New York: Penguin Books, 1998).

Figure 1.1 Umberto in January 1994. On the wall is a clipping from a newspaper article about him titled "I will tell the truth."

in this part of his narrative would sound familiar to anybody who has read other soldiers' accounts, regardless of their geographic and chronological focus. However, his description of the chaos and panic of defeat also specifically drew on a Russian representational canon—a Russian Text—that had taken shape after the overthrow of Napoleon's Grande Armée and ever since informed the ways in which Western writers discussed failed attacks on Russia.[18] This canon emphasized the deadly freeze, the blizzards, the glacial nights, and the snaps of frost. It described how the chill destroyed the last vestiges of military order, and how sickness, hunger, and

---

[18]Julien Sapori, *Marcher ou mourir: Les troupes italiennes on Russie 1941–1943* (Tours: Edition Sutton, 2018). On how literary articulations of the experience of war are inscribed in the memories of entire generations, see Paul Fussel, *The Great War and Modern Memory* (New York: Oxford University Press, 1975).

constant Russian harassment exhausted the columns of retreating soldiers. In this Russian Text, corpses frozen solid to the ground were plundered by those who followed after them as soldiers lost both all sense of pity and their mental sanity. Oblivious to their whereabouts and resembling ghostly figures, the survivors were represented as roaming across the landscape in a state of complete delirium, looking for something to eat and ready to fight with beastly fury over some slop or sunflower seeds. Without fail, this Text also mentioned the merciful "Russian" peasants who gave shelter to the soldiers adrift in the vast steppe.[19] Either consciously or unconsciously, Umberto's account of his "calvary" followed in the tradition of other Italian soldiers-memoirists in relying on this collective narrative, borrowing its narratological elements, and applying them to his personal story.

Then, besides literary conventions, underpinning Umberto's reminiscences was also a set of common anxieties that have marked the condition of the twentieth-century witnessing survivor.[20] In particular, beyond the already mentioned unforgettability of war and the simultaneous impossibility to recount it in any linear and rational manner, Umberto's recollections were informed by a fairly standard eyewitness's fear of being misunderstood and by a classic survivor's sense of guilt for having escaped death. Witnesses are skeptical about their audience's ability to understand their testimony because they assume that outsiders are not able to suspend disbelief and accept that completely abnormal events constituted the normality of a narrator's past life.[21] Umberto, too, felt the difficulty of making the abnormal he had experienced in the past accessible to individuals living in Bolzano in the 1990s. He wrote:

> Those who did not live through those harrowing moments, hours, and days might read these lines like they would read a play. Certainly, they would feel pity, but they would not

---

[19]See "Selected Further Readings."

[20]Ibid.

[21]Lawrence Langer, *Holocaust Testimonies: The Ruins of Memory* (New Haven, CT: Yale University Press, 1991).

truly understand—and that is not their fault. It is impossible to understand what cannot be explained. I would myself consider it impossible, had I not experienced it first-hand.[22]

Umberto dreaded that his future readers might use his memoirs simply as the starting point of a friendly chat, "comfortably sitting in their armchairs, with a cup of coffee in their hands," smiling affably at each other as though they were in a literary café. In response to this fear, he advocated the intention to depict each episode of his Soviet life—"tragic and less tragic, serious and silly"—precisely as he had experienced it. In so doing, he once again placed himself within a long-standing tradition of writing and reading memoirs, according to which testimonies become true stories only if bestowed with the value of a living memory. Bruner has called it "the discourse of witness" and explained that this type of narration strives to create "existential immediacy" and factuality.[23] Umberto's obsessive writing fits well with this poetics of evidence since his collection of written materials aimed to create veracity by virtue of authenticity. Yet, veracity does not relieve the witnessing survivor from his feeling of guilt. The act of remembering and writing, Umberto wrote, "weights on me, oppresses me, and causes me additional suffering. I shall consider it the sentence I must serve and the price I must pay for having survived."[24] For many Europeans, especially after the horrors of the Holocaust, these feelings encapsulate the inexplicability and ineffability of events in which life and death lost their solemnity and evil became banal.

Umberto's narrative, however, began to diverge from most other war and internment memoirs when it shifted to his stay at Zubova. The POW camps of the Second World War varied greatly, including considerable variation across the camps in the Western European theater of war. Some prisoners remembered relatively humane

---

[22]UM, "Reminescenze."

[23]Bruner, "The Autobiographical Process," 45.

[24]UM, "Reminescenze," and Commenti 30.10.1993 and 26.8.1994.

environments, while others recalled horrific conditions.[25] Nonetheless, amidst the great breadth of internees' memories, Soviet captivity has been quite consistently narrated as an experience of malnutrition, disease, and harsh labor when remaining alive was a daily fight. In Italy, the National Union of Veterans of Russia (UNIRR) established and propagated this narrative by means of its *Notiziario* [Newsletter]. Data found in the Soviet archives in the 1990s confirmed it. For instance, according to Soviet estimates reported by Scotoni, from a total of 68,564 Italian casualties, 19,043 died during the transfers to the camps and another 27,683 died in the camps and hospitals due to injuries and disease, while only 21,274 servicemen returned home alive after internment.[26] Other historians have also described the fate of Italian soldiers in Soviet captivity as particularly brutal. Those who did not die during the transfers were utterly exhausted and sick when they arrived at the camps and were forcefully integrated into the Gulag. There, the deprivations and strenuous labor imposed by the Soviet authorities as well as widespread bureaucratic inefficiency and corruption resulted in high death rates.[27] Against this background, Umberto's account stood out as especially unusual and unfamiliar: its structure, intention, symbols, and semantics were *not* those of a victim's story.

The former Italian POW did not denounce any physical abuse ever perpetrated to him or other prisoners. Quite the opposite, he insisted that no inhumane practices were inflicted on them. The appalling interrogations, tortures, humiliations, injuries, and harassments described by others never took place at Zubova, as he described it. In Umberto's narrative, prisoners were well taken care of, their living conditions progressively improved over the course of their internment, and some of them enjoyed liaisons with the hospital's nurses. In

---

[25]S.P. Mackenzie, "The treatment of prisoners of war in World War II," *The Journal of Modern History* 66, no. 3 (1994): 487–520; and Bob Moore, "The Treatment of Prisoners of War in the Western European Theatre of War, 1939–45," in *Prisoners in War*, ed. Sibylle Scheipers (New York: Oxford University Press, 2010), 111–25.

[26]Giorgio Scotoni, *L'Armata Rossa e la disfatta italiana (1942–1943)* (Trento: Panorama, 2007), 477.

[27]See "Selected Further Readings."

other words, while other survivors equated Soviet internment to a tomb where soldiers were cut off from the outside world and any positive personal transformation occurred only as a result of endured suffering, for Umberto the prisoners' hospital was a place of respite, rescue, and regeneration. His three years there were a time of political and personal growth, during which he understood the deceptiveness of fascist propaganda and learned from "the Russians" how to "forgive and love."[28]

When Umberto remembered Zubova, besides the content of his writing, his form significantly changed, too. While his war memories were about despair, hunger, thirst, and other raw emotions and sensations beyond logic, the recollections on internment were more distinctly about individual people and their relationships with Umberto. Although still loaded with personal commentary, they abounded in descriptions of ironic and grotesque incidents, which the narrator seemed to remember fondly. Here, memory became nostalgia: sweeter, gentler, and more enjoyable than what life had been.

A key "character" in this process was Zubova's political commissar, whom Umberto simply called Sergei. Soviet POW hospitals were managed by officers of the Ministry of Internal Affairs (NKVD) who responded directly to their bosses in all matters concerning prisoners' daily regimen and surveillance.[29] Umberto remembered Zubova's officer as "a crystalline and fundamentally sincere man" who followed the rules of evidence in meting out punishments and who satisfied Umberto's great curiosity and desire to learn. Although Umberto retrospectively might have understood that Sergei was an agent of Soviet indoctrination, in his writings he described him as somebody who pushed him to reflect and critically revisit many of his assumptions about both the Soviet Union and fascist Italy. As Umberto wrote, the political commissar "wanted to teach me the theories of Marx and

---

[28]AS, Umberto to Anfisa 18.5.1994.

[29]See decrees dated March 6 and April 12, 1943, in Vladimir Antonovich Zolotarev and Aleksandr Sergeevich Emelin, eds., *Russkii arkhiv: Velikaia Otechestvennaia: Inostrannye voennoplennye Vtoroi mirovoi voiny v SSSR*, T.24, (13) (Moscow: Terra, 1996), 80–1 and 100–2.

Lenin and we often argued, but, in the meantime, I saw that the theory of Fascism was bad and untruthful." The commissar was a convinced communist, but his communism, Umberto averred, "was not as bad as our cunning propaganda said."[30]

Many other individuals inhabiting Zubova's microcosm were portrayed in similarly positive terms. For instance, the NKVD sergeant commanding the hospital's guards, Umberto's "good comrade" Repkin, was recalled as a "gruff … but truly kind man," who, when not busy screaming at the German prisoners, liked to talk about women and brag about his seduction skills. Once, Montini and Repkin disagreed in their assessments of a nurse's beauty.

> He got mad, began to curse, and said: "You damned fascist, how can you be competent about women … ? How many ladies did you have in Italy?" I replied that my fiancé left me for another man and that's why I went far away to Russia. He became serious and pensive, and then said: "This is bad. This means that capitalist ladies are whores, too," and we laughed together.[31]

The story about the cheating fiancé was made up: young Umberto had several girlfriends before being mobilized but none of them was a serious affair. The point, however, is whether this way of joking with each other was possible between an ordinary POW and the commander of the guards. Was Umberto misrepresenting his relationship with Repkin to make a point about the goodness of the Soviet people? Or does his portrayal of Repkin reveal that Umberto was no ordinary prisoner, maybe even an informer or a collaborator involved in reeducation programs for the other POWs? Or, perhaps, all the above? Regardless of how we answer these questions, the quotation above highlights the nostalgic bond that Umberto felt toward Repkin. It is also significant that, until his death, Umberto deeply cherished the red star pin that Repkin had put in his pocket

---

[30] UM, Commenti, 24.2.1994; AS, Umberto to Anfisa 29.6.1994 and 20.3.1995.
[31] UM, Commenti, 13.2.1994; and AS, Umberto to Anfisa 25.3.1994.

at the time of repatriation. He wrote, "That was Repkin: he appeared grim, grumpy, and always ready to yell offenses at us 'capitalists.' But this is how he showed his regret when we were repatriated. Certainly, that ferocious face was not the mirror of his soul. Deep down he, too, was good."[32]

Umberto recognized that, throughout the years of internment, both he and his companions had felt various degrees of skepticism, depression, and apathy toward recovery. These emotions were part of his "discourse of witness." But they also represented a narrative problem. How could he explain these negative feelings while also maintaining the depiction of Zubova as a site of attentive care? His writings on this subject were highly contradictory and revealing of his inner struggles. Ultimately, however, they reconciled the contrast between prisoners' "moral suffering" and their experience of care by blaming circumstances which did not undermine Umberto's claim about the Soviet people's compassion. Key among these circumstances was fascist propaganda. According to it, "the Russians" were "a nation of bloodthirsty troglodytes," who would shoot any prisoner upon capture.[33] Having been fed this line throughout their young lives, the Italian soldiers could not make sense of why they were not shot on the spot but rather taken to a hospital. In turn, lack of comprehension caused psychological infirmities. Yet, Umberto insisted, these fears and the depression that came with them were "unfounded" and "unjustified" because no mistreatment had actually happened. As he claimed, "it should have been enough to look at the situation in which we lived [i.e. a hospital] to chase away any pessimistic foreboding."[34] In other words, as opposed to his war narrative with its emphasis on the profound character of his traumas during the exceptional shocks of retreat and capture, Umberto's captivity narrative related as banal and normalized the ongoing traumas of his internment. Any deeply

---

[32]UM, Commenti 11.4.1994.

[33]On this, see also Quinto Antonelli, ed., "La Campagna di Russia (1941–1943). Lettere, Diari, Memorie," in *"La propaganda e' l'unica nostra cultura". Scritture autobiografiche dal fronte sovietico (1941–1943)* (Trento: Fondazione Museo Storico Trentino, 2016), 9–58.

[34]UM, Commenti 7.5.1993 and 5.7.1993.

intense moment of psychological crisis was just recorded within the routine flow of everyday life.

The fact that Umberto was spared the violence of exploitation that ruled in the Soviet labor camps, being instead assigned to a POW hospital, is a slim explanation for his positive memory of captivity. Living conditions in POW hospitals—like in other medical facilities for unprofitable prisoners subordinate to the NKVD—were merciless. Camp authorities did not care much about the lives of their sick captives, and the therapeutic efforts of a few doctors were made irrelevant by their powerlessness in the camp hierarchy, the primitive medical means at their disposal, and the inadequate food rations of the wartime. As the historian Golfo Alexopoulos has written, these facilities were in all effects just "dumping ground[s]" where the NKVD sent the sickest prisoners to die.[35] Rather than Umberto's stay in a hospital, I see two different but interconnected reasons behind the unusual features of his internment testimony.

The first reason is based in his experience and the exceptionally privileged condition he enjoyed as intermediary between Soviet authorities and Italian POWs. Serving as the hospital's interpreter (perhaps even as the commissar's collaborator) and being sustained by Polina's affection shaped what he remembered and how he recounted his story. His were the memories of a man who had received Soviet political re-education and, being particularly receptive to it after the experience of military defeat, accepted to view his captivity as a time of catharsis and personal maturation. They were also the recollections of a person who had fallen in love during internment. Certainly, we might question the consensual nature of his relationship with one of his captors. Nonetheless, his nostalgic longing for his youth in the Soviet Union affected the sympathetic gaze with which he looked back and provided a sentimental background for many of his observations.

---

[35]Golfo Alexopoulos, *Illness and Inhumanity in Stalin's Gulag* (New Haven, CT: Yale University Press, 2017), 162.

The second reason behind the distinctiveness of Umberto's memory of Zubova is related to authorial intent, that is the author's deliberate task and the agenda that drove his project of public commemoration. Umberto was committed to proving three main points on the grounds of his embodied experience: 1. the "unjustified, absurd, and scandalous" character of the Second World War and the "ineptitude" of the Italian army's High Command during it; 2. the unfairness of Italy's postwar "democratic justice" as the disabled veterans received only "ridiculous handouts" as compensation for their sacrifices; and 3. the "humanity" with which the "so-called barbarous Russians" had treated him and other POWs.[36] In line with the first point, Umberto's war testimony was both a criticism of Italian military strategy *and* a moral judgment, a questioning of the righteousness of the war into which Mussolini had pushed Italy. Instead, his sanitized description of the hospital's workings as a Soviet institution betrayed his commitment to the third argument.

One might think that Umberto had internalized the Soviet-imposed antifascist narrative of victimhood at the hands of Fascism/Nazism and political redemption during captivity in the USSR. At this narrative's heart lay a view of Soviet captivity as a site of regeneration where the POWs recognized their guilt for having fought in the fascist armies.[37] Italian communist converts such as Danilo Ferretti and Giuseppe Lamberti had embraced this narrative and produced "singular" accounts of Soviet captivity due to their "blind belief in communism."[38] Crucial for Umberto, however, was the mandate to pay a "debt of gratitude." His was a personal more than strictly political loyalty, one grounded in the human bonds he had established and on a rather thin antifascist ideological foundation.

In light of this, we should see Umberto not only as a witness-bearing testimony but also as a potential source of misinformation,

---

[36]UM, "Sorvolando."

[37]Wienand, *Returning Memories*; and Frank Biess, *Homecomings: Returning POWs and the Legacies of Defeat in Postwar Germany* (Princeton, NJ: Princeton University Press, 2006).

[38]Giusti, "Dal fascismo al communism," 153 and 156.

creating through his narration an idealized version of both "Russia" and himself. Like other soldiers-memoirists, the elderly, traumatized veteran portrayed himself as an authoritative narrator telling us a "true" story. Although at times he recognized the nostalgic nature of his memory, he insistently claimed to be "unbiased" in laying out his experiences.[39] Conversations with other former POWs were essential to him because, so Umberto believed, they confirmed and validated the "truthfulness" of his memories. At the same time, however, Umberto's text also challenges his authority as a narrator because his readers see him confused and suffering from psychological trauma. In addition, both his sense of guilt—having survived thanks to his cushy position in the hospital—and his specific purpose—to make us accept the essential goodness of the "Russian" people—compelled him to withhold, manipulate, distort, or disguise information, imaginatively transforming or repressing and denying memories that did not fit with the narrative he wanted to shape.

The Correspondence with Anfisa

Shortly after Umberto's RAI UNO appearance and the sad news he received in that venue about Polina's death, an unexpected companion joined him on his journey of remembrance and narration—a former employee of the prisoners' hospital named Anfisa Alekseevna Serzhanina. Having found each other by a veritable twist of fate, the two began holding an intensely emotional correspondence that straddled the line between memory of the past and reflection on the present. Their exchange has been pivotal in my attempt to reconstruct Umberto's wartime and post-repatriation experience because this set of sources does not simply echo his memoirs but rather complements and elucidates them in significant ways. The contrast between the milieu in which Umberto lived (the Northern Italian provincial town of Bolzano with its relative affluence and peacefulness) and the more

---

[39]UM, Commenti, 30.10.1993.

difficult environment of Anfisa's life (the Ural city of Perm' in the mid-1990s) pushed the two correspondents to explain themselves to each other, which, in turn, generated more commentary about past events than was the case in Umberto's recollections. Besides differences of geography and political context, however, their correspondence was shaped also by a sense of personal intimacy due to the years they both spent at Zubova.

Born in 1923, Anfisa had barely graduated from a technical institute, when, in 1943, she moved to Zubova with her 1-year-old daughter Tamara. Her husband had been stationed in Moscow as a military driver after having suffered an injury at the front, and she chose to move to the town of Zubova both because her in-laws lived there and because it was deep enough in the Soviet rear to make her feel safe. Unable to find employment in her field, Anfisa took up a job in the prisoners' hospital as attendant and manager of the clothing warehouse, an appointment that lasted two years and allowed her to make Umberto's acquaintance. Then, in 1953, she and her demobilized husband moved to Perm'. There, she had two more children and landed a job as chief engineer in a local factory, thus becoming too busy to spend much time dwelling on the memory of the prisoners' hospital.

The re-connection with the world of Zubova Poliana happened for Anfisa only at the beginning of 1992 when she applied for new pension benefits. Although she had officially retired in 1978, with the post-1991 reform of the pensioning system she needed to collect documents testifying to her working record, including the two years she had worked at the POWs' hospital. Aware that this type of certificate could hardly be obtained by mail but unwilling to undertake the long trip from her residence in Perm' to the small Mordovian town of Zubova Poliana, she sent her son-in-law Vladimir to get the document for her. From Mordovia, however, Vladimir brought back not only a copy of Anfisa's working record but also a letter that Umberto had sent to Zubova in search for his beloved Polina and that had ended up in the city's military commissariat. Since neither the hospital nor the local authorities had any record of where the evacuated personnel had gone after the war, the military commissar had been unable to provide an answer to Umberto's enquiry. Now, looking at Anfisa's file and seeing that Doctor Ovodkova had been her supervisor, he handed Umberto's letter to Vladimir: perhaps his mother-in-law knew something and would be able to assist this Italian man in his quest. In fact, Anfisa had not been privy to Polina's whereabouts (let alone to the fact that Polina had already passed away). Yet she remembered Umberto very clearly because he and other Italian prisoners used to play with her daughter while she worked at the hospital. According to what she wrote to Umberto in her very first letter to him, it was precisely the positive memory of these young men and the desire to know "where they are now" that prompted her to write to him.[40]

Umberto and Anfisa were reconnected serendipitously. But there is more than chance to the story of how Vladimir entered the office of Zubova's military commissar asking for a declaration about Anfisa's employment and the commissar suggested Anfisa might help Umberto find news about Doctor Ovodkova. This story reflects the changed world in which Russian citizens lived in the early 1990s. While all the letters that Umberto had sent to the Soviet Union in the previous thirty years were stopped by the censors (or at least he thought so) and never received an answer, after the communist government's collapse the exchange of letters between Russian citizens and foreigners was no longer censored. Such a radical change seemed improbable to Umberto. His experience as a POW had taught him that both possessing information and delivering it to Westerners was dangerous for the local population. As he wrote, "people could get in trouble just by showing that they knew something." Suspicious of the real scope of the changes brought by perestroika and the fall of the Soviet Union, Umberto considered "the political situation in Russia" to be "still very confused," with the "KGB's sinister shadow" still lingering over the country.[41] Thus, he was surprised by what he perceived to be Anfisa's lack of caution and shocked that she sent him the address of a state archive where he could find information about Polina's demobilization.

---

[40]UM, Anfisa to Umberto, 20.2.1993.
[41]UM, "Deduzioni."

And yet, despite these initial misgivings, the correspondence with Anfisa quickly became vital to him. He wrote to her even after an operation in his right eye and the doctor's prescription not to read or write; he also regularly sent her money to make sure her postage expenses were covered and she did not have reasons to stop writing. His letters betrayed his desperate desire for emotional intimacy with a person from his past. Anfisa, on her end, did not need financial encouragement to write since she and her family were eager to enjoy the newly acquired freedom to talk with Westerners. As she wrote, "When I receive a letter from you, we always have a little celebration. My children and grandchildren are very interested in our correspondence, especially enjoying the postcards and photographs you send."[42]

Most importantly, to both Anfisa and Umberto, this correspondence brought "great joy" and "pleasure" because it allowed them to remember their wartime youth in positive terms and indulge in their nostalgia.[43] Letter upon letter, they not only described the suffering that had marked their lives but also longingly discussed political values and cultural tastes that they shared but could no longer see in their present. For instance, they both liked old Russian folk songs (many of which Umberto had learned from Polina during his internment); adhered to traditional ideas of femininity and masculinity; and complained about contemporary youth's lost capacity to work efficiently. Nostalgic about the past, they misconstrued and simplified it, often using it as a yardstick to measure the alleged mistakes of the present.[44]

Indeed, albeit to different extents and in different ways, both Umberto and Anfisa were stuck in the past and evoked it through episodes to which they still felt tethered. For instance, when Umberto received Anfisa's first letter, he could not recall her. In a successive

---

[42]UM, Anfisa to Umberto 2.7.1993.

[43]These terms come up in multiple letters. See, for instance, UM, Anfisa to Umberto 30.10.1993.

[44]See also Peter Fritzsche, "How Nostalgia Narrates Modernity," in *The Work of Memory: New Directions in the Study of German Society and Culture*, ed. Alan Confino and Peter Fritzsche (Urbana: University of Illinois Press, 2002), 62–85.

letter, however, she reminded him of a curious incident that had happened in the hospital, and, thanks to this, he was able to "perfectly identify her in [his] visual memory." Later, when he began to call her on the phone, he also remembered her voice, and the "music" of her Russian immediately brought him back to his "green years." Along with the photographs, postcards, and newspaper cutouts that they sent each other and that they both avidly assembled, Anfisa's letters provided fuel for Umberto's memory project: the individuals and episodes she mentioned "orient[ed]" his memory, prompting him to remember details he had forgotten.[45] Places, too, played an important role in their letters: as Anfisa and Umberto reminisced about their wanderings within the hospital and through its fenced borders, their correspondence opened up Zubova's mysteries. Furthermore, since unlike other survivors Umberto was never able to go on a physical "memory journey" to Russia, the letter exchange vicariously allowed him to visualize and conquer the space of his internment, which in turn led Umberto to an excavation of his inner world.

Like the conversations Umberto began to have with other former POWs after his television appearance, Anfisa's letters functioned for him as witness evidence: they were a confirmation of that "truth" that he so desperately wanted to make public. Unlike the testimonies of other eyewitness, in Umberto's opinion, Anfisa's words had the additional power of coming from "the Russian depths" and "from a person who deserves much more esteem than [Italian] lying journalists." He believed that the letters from Perm' could not be possibly instrumentalized for any political aim because they were part of a private correspondence and constituted a "100 percent truthful source of information." As this "typical everyday Russian woman" agreed with most of Umberto's memories and assessments on the Russian people, he considered her (and by extension any ordinary Russian) as more reliable and less ideologically brainwashed than his fellow Italians.[46]

---

[45]UM, "Deduzioni"; Commenti 30.11.1994 and 7.5.1993.
[46]UM, Commenti 16.10.1993 and untitled note dated January 1999; AS, Umberto to Anfisa 13.8.1994.

There was little respect in Umberto's writings for postwar Italy, which he described as "volatile and petty, scared by truths which could ideologically infect its unreflective, sheep-like people, and ready to do anything to loyally follow directives from overseas … including falsifying history." As he was concerned, the stories that circulated since the 1950s about POWs being killed and tortured in the Soviet Union were "lies" not supported by any evidence and divulged by individuals who just wanted to make a profit, while letting their story be used in support of American geopolitical interests. Having made the "wrong" choice to join NATO, Umberto claimed, the postwar Italian state had begun to "demonize" the Soviet order and its Marxist-Leninist ideology. As a result, "millions of 'smart' Italians" now believed that, since the Russians are communists, they must be "like wild animals, bad, and bloodthirsty." As he concluded with sarcasm, "we live in the country of liberties, where everything is allowed besides saying the truth."[47]

To Umberto, who not only scorned the Italian past but also "despise[d] this present" and was "disgusted by this world," contact with Anfisa gave the opportunity to glorify the Soviet past and apologetically mourn the end of its ideology. Despite his multiple claims of objectivity, his appraisal of key moments in Soviet history betrayed his political sympathies and the ability of the NKVD officer at Zubova to shape the ideas of this young man at a formative time in his life. For instance, Umberto likened communist ideology to "a medicine" and "a doctor," the only one who, at the beginning of the twentieth century, could bring the sick tsarist empire back to health. He wrote:

The October Revolution of 1917 liberated the Russians from a nightmare … The worker and the peasant could finally hold in their hands the weapons that they had until then feared … Albeit bloody at times, I think it was justified if we consider … the radicality of change and the positive consequences it had. The most important of them … is the huge victory of the Red Army

---

[47]UM, Commenti 16.10.1993; and AS, Umberto to Anfisa, 13.8.1994.

over the Nazi troops that had spread all over Europe. That war machine, as much perfect as ill-omened, had scared everybody and was stopped only by Russia. It was in Russia that Hitler lost the war![48]

This was exactly the narrative propagated by the Soviet state in the aftermath of the Second World War.[49] In it, any pre-war form of state violence was justified as the foundation that built a system which went on to save Europe from the Nazis' genocidal campaign. Having appropriated this narrative, Umberto averred that the Red Army's "great victory" and march to Berlin had been the determining factors in the defeat of Germany. The "Russians," he insisted with complete disregard for the multiethnic composition of the Red Army, had done their "sacred duty" by defending their country and "liberating Europe." Most crucially, they had not committed the wartime atrocities that other armies did, such as the carpet bombing of German cities done by the American and British aviation. "I cannot forget," Umberto wrote to Anfisa, "the German town of Dresden, through which I went on my way back from Russia. The Americans had bombed it so much and many women and children had died (the German women told me so). And then the Russian Red Army came. The Russians never bombed a city where there were only children and women!"[50] Didn't German women also tell Umberto about the Soviet soldiers' raping and pillaging? Or did Umberto forget that detail?

Umberto's assessment of Stalin similarly reveals the extent to which he had internalized the pre-Thaw Stalinist cult of personality, including the trope of people's gratitude to Stalin as great military leader and astute politician.[51]

---

[48]UM, "Deduzioni"; Commenti 30.10.1993, 30.1.1994, 24.2.1994, and 13.2.1994; AS, Umberto to Anfisa without date, probably Summer 1996.

[49]David L. Hoffmann, "Introduction: The Politics of Commemoration in the Soviet Union and Contemporary Russia," in *The Memory of the Second World War in Soviet and Post-Soviet Russia*, ed. David L. Hoffman (New York: Routledge, 2021), 1–14.

[50]UM, Commenti 22.6.1994; AS, Umberto to Anfisa 10.2.1994.

[51]Yan Mann, "Situating Stalin in the History of the Second World War," in *The Memory of the Second World War in Soviet and Post-Soviet Russia*, ed. David L. Hoffman (New York: Routledge, 2021), 41–63.

> If ... during that wretched ... march I cursed Stalin, later I thanked him for having fed me and cured me ... Besides being well prepared in military art, he was an excellent politician and master chess player ... It is a fact that he led Russia to a resounding victory ... In the end, I felt sympathy for that mustached Georgian as it was by his order that we were repatriated.[52]

Umberto's historical interpretation of the Cold War similarly echoed Soviet official discourses. In his view, after 1945 the American government had feared that the Soviet Union might stop the United States' expansion into Europe, and, for this reason, had instigated the beginning of a systemic confrontation with the USSR. Moreover, Umberto explained, it was not the victory of capitalism that had truly ended the Cold War but rather the grievous actions committed by Mikhail Gorbachev. The last Soviet leader had "sold Russia" to the Americans and inflicted "traumas" upon his countrymen by implementing reforms that did "too much and too fast." Instead of praising Gorbachev's policy of *glasnost'* (openness) and the opportunity it gave the Soviet people to reflect critically on their past, Umberto wished that ordinary citizens had never learned about the "crimes" their country had committed. In addition, Umberto strongly condemned Gorbachev for supporting the withdrawal of Soviet troops from East Germany and "giving freedom" to the non-Russian Soviet Republics. "Truly," Umberto summed up his thoughts in a note,

> I did not like the course history took [under Gorbachev] and still do not like it ... I understand that it was necessary to do some touch-ups ... but it was an infelicitous choice to destroy all that had that lasted more than 70 years and had shown positive outcomes.[53]

---

[52]UM, Commenti 24.2.1994.
[53]UM, Commenti 13.2.1994 and 8.3.1994; AS, Umberto to Anfisa 20.3.1995.

As Umberto's correspondence with Anfisa developed, Polina—who was dead and could not have a say in how either letter-writer reconstructed the past—became a proxy to support his portrayal of the "Russian people" as a kindhearted nation ready to help anybody and able to answer hatred with love. Of course, this pleased Anfisa. Although she had not been indifferent to the fate of the POWs and still remembered their tears, she also lacked the desire to question her country's past, "the fascist war," and her own life before and after Zubova. Umberto's memory of his experience as POW confirmed the positive narrative she wanted to preserve. Thus, on July 5, 1993, Anfisa thanked him "for understanding the Russians so well. We do not wish evil upon anybody and even if we are wronged, we are able to forgive." On February 24, 1994, she repeated this point: "How many of our husbands and fathers died! But despite this, we did not hurt any single foreigner. The Germans instead burned in their crematories our women, children, and elderly people." On August 26, 1994, congratulating Umberto for his "battle" with the Italian state for the sake of the Russian people, she argued: "those who have come close to the Russian people will never say that the Russians are wild beasts. And the communists … they were all different. Perhaps, some of them were indeed ruthless, but most were normal people." As for the purges of the 1930s, Anfisa squarely put the blame on "local authorities," while Stalin for her remained a strict but capable leader.[54]

Many of Anfisa's letters include familiar clichés of this type, which she employed both to reinforce Umberto's (a foreigner!) already positive view of her country and to understand her own life trajectory. Illustrative is a letter in which she sketched out her biography in stereotypical terms of hardship, resilience, the dignifying power of labor, and the Soviet people's endless capacity to both make sacrifices and enjoy life.

I remember my youth. I was an orphan but could nonetheless study. I wore poor clothes and shoes and was always hungry, but

---

[54]UM, Anfisa to Umberto, 5.7.1993, 24.2.1994, 26.8.1994, and 1.6.1996.

I had fun in my free time: I went to dances and concerts, and I always smiled. I don't remember myself sad, apart from the days when my parents died, first my dad when I was 10 and then my mom when I was 15. Still very young, I began to work in a kolkhoz during the holidays. I cut the grass, harvested the rye and the wheat, and did all sorts of agricultural work. This is why I could easily bear loneliness and, after the death of my husband, raise my children alone, always being happy. My work sustained me. I was appreciated there. They put me on the board of honor and helped me materially in raising my children.[55]

As Anfisa clarified in other letters, her father was a wealthy peasant, a *kulak*, whose entire property was confiscated by the state in the collectivization campaign of 1929 and who served a four-year sentence in a labor camp for his class origins. Yet, the elderly woman remembered these events not as wrongs done to her but as struggles that forged her character.[56]

In contrast to the soul searching and history rewriting in which some of her contemporaries engaged since the mid-1980s, Anfisa did not feel any need to rethink her country's historical narrative or repudiate the ideology that had given meaning to her life. Quite the opposite, as she struggled with both her family's problems (such as her son's alcoholism) and her country's economic and identity crises, the Soviet past remained a source of pride for her. She complained, "but now, with democracy, there is no longer anything good"—neither job security for graduating students, nor consumer goods at low prices or safety on the streets. It was not a coincidence that, when the economic and social fabric of her country broke down in early 1995, her laments about the present became even stronger. She wrote,

Before it was better: we all had equal rights. But now whoever can steal or speculate gets rich, while the pensioners or the

---

[55]UM, Anfisa to Umberto, 30.1.1994.
[56]UM, Anfisa to Umberto, 30.5.1994 and 9.10.1995.

single mothers become poor and even turn into beggars. Now you must pay for education and medical care, while before everything was free. Before, every year I went to a resort to restore my health, but now it is impossible for me. All the simple people curse Gorbachev for his perestroika.

Criminals roam through the country. People stopped working; the factories stand idle; alcoholism runs high … Before, if a person did not work for more than two months, he was held accountable, but now there are young men who don't work for years and nobody is bothered by that … Personally, I don't like today's government … today's anarchy will not lead anywhere good.[57]

In Anfisa's opinion, it was because of the new capitalists' incapacity to rule the country—their "immorality, boorishness, power struggles, scrounging, and banditism"—that "the simple people" missed communism and were eager to vote for the communist party.[58] Living in an unpredictable present and feeling uneasy in the face of her country's political and economic transformation, Anfisa looked back at the Soviet Union with an uncritically nostalgic gaze.

In the end, Anfisa and Umberto's letters testify to two diverging national cultures of memory. Hers fit well with other scholars' findings about the so-called transition of the 1990s. Namely, that the insecurities of that decade ensured both people's dissatisfaction with the current social order and nostalgia for an implausibly harmonious Soviet past and the unquestioning moral authority of communist ideology. They also reflect the pride of a country that came out victorious in the Second World War.[59] His, instead, are the memories of a defeated veteran who rejected his country's past, recognized his mistakes in believing in Mussolini's propaganda, and dissociated himself from the

---

[57]UM, Anfisa to Umberto, 5.1.1995 and 13.3.1995.

[58]UM, Anfisa to Umberto, 6.12.1995 and 4.4.1996.

[59]See, for instance, Svetlana Alexievich, *Second-Hand Time* (New York: Random House, 2016).

fascist cause.[60] Umberto wrote, "we went to that land to do evil against people who are better than us … I am ashamed that I was part of that war, that I was guilty of premeditated aggression …" In this context, as neither Italy's postwar history nor its present provided any relief to Umberto's sense of culpability, the only solace left for him seemed to be in his nostalgia for the Soviet Union. Over the years, he kept cultivating the delusional thought that "Russia" was and continued to be a "poor and unfortunate" country populated by people who had chosen to repudiate war and believed in peace "without political or territorial aims." When faced with the news of a war in Chechnya in 1994–5, Umberto could not offer any political commentary on the events. He only lamented the "falling" of his "dear Russia" into yet another war and, as per his habit, attacked the Italian media for politicizing this conflict to shed negative light on Russia.[61] I wonder how elderly Umberto would have responded to the Russian annexation of Crimea in 2014 and its full-scale invasion of Ukraine in 2022.

* * *

When Umberto finished recording all "episodes" he could possibly remember, he sought a literary executor ready to sort out his scattered memories, turn them into a narrative, and help him publish them as a book. He contacted Flavia Filippi, a distant cousin from neighboring Trento who had studied Russian language in college and then married a historian of the Soviet Union with whom she frequently traveled to Russia (my dear friend Giorgio Scotoni). The couple seemed the perfect candidates to whip Umberto's writings into shape under his close guidance. He wrote to Anfisa, "finally, I have found convincing and solid allies." Yet, after some initial enthusiasm, prickly and irascible Umberto met their work with increasing hostility and complained that they were not doing as they were bid.[62]

---

[60]Jochen Hellbeck, "Remembering Stalingrad," *Raritan: A Quarterly Review* 31, no. 4 (Spring 2012): 134–47.

[61]UM, Commenti 30.1.1994 and 28.3.1994; AS, Umberto to Anfisa 9.1.1995 and 20.3.1995.

[62]AS, Umberto to Anfisa, 29.5.1996 and 9.8.1996; author's correspondence with Giorgio Scotoni dated July 8, 2023.

Similar setbacks followed one after the other, but Umberto did not let them stop him. Looking for the right editor to "get it published," he distributed copies of his writings to other family friends, including the Bolzano resident Corrado Palmarin.[63] In 2023, twenty years after Umberto's death, Palmarin accomplished the task Umberto had entrusted to him and finally published his notes under the romanticized title *Among the Sunflowers and Under the Birch Trees*. What had been a set of discrete, highly fragmented recollections turned into a first-person narrative—grammatically corrected and streamlined but also semi-fictionalized and including several historical inaccuracies.[64] As a result of this book, Umberto's voice found some public echo and his "truth," as he had hoped for, survived his own death.[65]

Yet, the complicated dilemmas that underpinned this former POW's aspiration to remember, narrate, and heal, while also fighting against "any slander and political lie" about Russia remained buried in his personal archive.[66] Concealed also remained his position as active subject, participating in both fascist and Soviet politics, perhaps willing to inform and collaborate in the camp or (I would ultimately suggest) just opportunistically trying to survive and even help his mates.[67] Having gone to war in a mood of exalted self-sacrifice, Umberto returned home feeling betrayed by Mussolini's fascist propaganda and with his pre-war beliefs changed by the Soviet propaganda he had internalized at Zubova. I see my role as helping rescue from obscurity precisely these sides of Umberto's story and injured Self, aiming through them to illuminate wider traumas and political beliefs of European twentieth-century history.

---

[63]UM, Anfisa to Umberto, 9.10.1995.

[64]Corrado Palmarin, *In Mezzo ai Girasoli e Sotto le Betulle* (Acqui Terme: Impressioni Grafiche, 2023).

[65]Roberto Brumat, "La ritirata, l'orrore e i girasoli. Una storia da raccontare," *Corriere del Trentino*, March 8, 2023, 2.

[66]AS, Umberto to Anfisa, 28.2.1996.

[67]Letters from fellow former prisoners confirm that Umberto tried to help them as much as he could. See, for instance, Museo Storico Italiano della Guerra, uncatalogued Fondo Umberto Montini, letter from Mariano Ruggeri dated October 14, 1994.

CHAPTER 2
FASCIST YOUTH AND THE CALL
TO ARMS

Most of Umberto Montini's countrymen in the 1930s would have called him a good young fascist—optimistic and enthusiastic but also disciplined and deferential to authority, always conforming to the rules set by state and family. Through the development of strong ties of association with the fascist nation, by his late teens Umberto had largely identified with Fascism. He had cultivated a fascist working ethos and become morally prepared for waging war on its behalf. With sports and study as his only interests, he appeared to personify one of the then popular slogans: "*libro e moschetto—fascista perfetto*" ("book and rifle—perfect fascist"). As historians, however, we might have a more nuanced view of him. Rather than a "perfect fascist," Umberto was an ordinary young man whose judgments about Fascism expressed the mixed responses of many other Italian youths to the cult of disciple and their country's militarization. On the one hand, he felt the pull of war's excitement and his elation at the coming of war was part of fascist Italy's mood. On the other hand, once in the barracks, Umberto confronted plummeting morale as an increasing number of people around him were reacting to war with alarm and dismay. In addition, he chafed under the yoke of military hierarchy and, against the fascist rhetoric of disciplined subjugation, was on occasion willing to disobey orders and brave his superiors' wrath. Reconstructing Umberto's pre-Second World War and pre-Russia life, this chapter gauges the depth and the limits of a young fascist's enthusiasm and obedience within the context of Italy's increasing mobilization for war.

An Obedient and Politically Naïve Young Man

Growing up, Umberto had been a member of all organizations managed by the Opera Nazionale Balilla, the fascist youth agency founded by Benito Mussolini in 1926. More than once he had the "honor" to represent Bolzano at the national sport events *Dux* camps in Rome, where the young *avanguardisti* of the fascist state showcased their athletic skills.[1] He may have skipped school a few times, but he had never missed his Saturday pre-military courses. This training, which was intended to improve the spiritual and physical quality of future recruits, was mandatory for all Italian men between the ages of seventeen and twenty. It fit with the fascist political objectives of national revival, vigor, affirmation, and total social mobilization to unleash a war of conquest. Combined with sports, this training helped create those New Italians, whom party secretary Augusto Turati described in 1928 as ever thinking about "the hour of victory and of battle."[2] Through it, Umberto, like many Italians of his generation, was initiated into the political world of Fascism and learned to appreciate its aggregating force. He enjoyed fascist activities, found them stimulating, and supported their unforgiving militarism.

Umberto was also an obedient son, who deferred to his elders' authority and was respectful of the "natural" hierarchies of generation and class. When he finished middle school, his father told him that he could no longer support his education due to their family's economic situation. Augusto Montini used to work in a print shop, but the owner had fired him because of his socialist political leanings and his unwillingness to join the local fascist party. Indeed, membership in the party became a discriminating factor for employment in the mid-1930s, when having a party card was made obligatory for many categories of workers. On top of that, this was the time of the Great Depression, which affected the Montinis like million other families, and Augusto struggled to find a stable and solid source of income.

---

[1] UM, "Descrizione."

[2] Augusto Turati, *Il partito e i suoi compiti* (Roma: Libreria della Littoria, 1928), 147.

Umberto understood that his duty as a son was to find a job. Although he liked school and was saddened that he could not continue his studies, Umberto was proud to be able to help his family.

Thus, sometime in the mid- to late 1930s, young Montini dutifully entered the world of work. He found a job as office boy and assistant debt collector at the state holding institute INA but quickly realized that he did not like it and began to look for ways to quit. The opportunity arose when the firm Oskar Bondy opened a position for a bilingual, Italo-German shorthand typist. Founded in 1906 by the eponymous Jewish entrepreneur, the Oskar Bondy was a large import-export company dealing in tanning leathers and fur skins.[3] Umberto did not know how to type, but nonetheless showed up for the job interview and, at the end of it, walked out with an offer in hand. It helped that German was native to him (he had learned it from his Austrian mother) and that Signorina Erminia, an old unmarried woman working for the company, secretly whispered instructions to him during the mandatory typing test.

At the Oskar Bondy, we are told in his memoirs, Umberto's apprenticeship in the professional world progressed well. He worked diligently and, soon enough, was able to distinguish between various furs. Besides typing, he also helped at the switchboard answering the many telephone calls that came in from all over Europe. Around him, he heard other employees speak in German, Italian, Croatian, Slovene, Spanish, and English. The company's director, Oskar Bondy's nephew Karl Bondy, was fluent in all these languages, and Umberto looked up to him with admiration. He was captivated by this stern man who treated him with a mix of gentleness and discipline, called him "Signor Montini" despite his young age, and taught him to always be on time. At the end of the first month of work Umberto thanked Karl for his paycheck, but the director responded: "it is us who should thank *You*." Karl's formal way of addressing him ("*Lei*") made Umberto feel like he was somebody. It was a measure of deference that had a middle-class

---

[3]Joachim Innerhofer and Sabine Mayr, *Mörderische Heimat: verdrängte Lebensgeschichten jüdischer Familien in Bozen und Meran* (Bozen: Edition Raetia, 2015), 282.

value to him, distinguished him from his blue-collar father, and made him leave the office every day feeling happy.

At home, his parents were pleased, too, because the Oskar Bondy paid good salaries. Umberto handed over to them all the money he made, and they rewarded him by leaving with him a small amount to "take girls to the movies." Like most other young bachelors of his time, Umberto enjoyed the modern pastime of going to the cinema. However, he also strove to invest his disposable income in different pursuits, such as taking private French language classes at the then well-known Berlitz school.

Proud of himself and convinced that all was going well, Umberto was surprised—or so he remembers—to notice disquieting changes at work toward the end of 1938. His employers' faces stopped having their usual calm and controlled joviality. Karl looked worried and when Signorina Erminia chattered with the warehouse manager Heinz, it seemed like they did not want Umberto to understand. They did not push him away but behaved as though they wanted to protect him from knowing something. When he confided this observation to his father, he received a curt and simple explanation: the Bondys were Jews, were persecuted by the government, and would soon have to leave the country.

Although some scholars debate the extent to which ordinary Italians approved of their country's official anti-Semitism, all agree that throughout 1938 the Italian state's anti-Jewish stance became increasingly evident. In July of that year, a "racial manifesto" proclaimed that the Jews did not belong to the Italian race, and in September–November a set of racial laws introduced discriminatory legislation against Italy's Jewish citizens.[4] Yet, in his recollections Umberto claims that he had neither been aware of nor internalized any anti-Semitic discourse. When Karl had asked him during the job interview how he felt about working for a Jewish company, Umberto

---

[4]Renzo De Felice, *Storia degli ebrei italiani sotto il fascismo* (Turin: Einaudi, 1988); and Alessandro Visani, "Italian reactions to the racial laws of 1938 as seen through the classified files of the Ministry of Popular Culture," *Journal of Modern Italian Studies* 11, no 2 (2006): 171–87.

had nonchalantly answered that he made no distinction between Italians and Jews. This answer had convinced Karl to offer him a job because it suggested that Umberto was not prejudiced against the Jews. Later, the explanation his father gave him regarding the change of atmosphere in the Oskar Bondy alerted Umberto to something he had allegedly not seen until then. Nonetheless, he remained unsure whether he should trust the "rumors" about Jewish discrimination. His hesitation, he emphasized in his writings, was a measure of how much he wanted to believe in the nobility of Mussolini's aims and Fascism's moral righteousness. Whether or not these were Umberto's sensibilities at that time and whether he was truly immune to the then widespread racial thinking, in the retrospective (post-Holocaust) recounting of his life, Umberto's surprise and disbelief about Jewish persecution signaled two important features of how he wanted to be perceived by his readers: his political naiveté and Fascism's failure to build up in him real support for anti-Semitic ideas.

Alongside changes at work, by the end of the 1930s, the atmosphere at home was shifting too, especially as Silvio Flor began to visit the Montinis house more frequently. Flor was a well-known South Tyrolean political activist, who had belonged to the Italian Communist Party before the onset of Fascism, had attended the International Lenin School in Moscow in 1933–6, and had then returned to Italy in 1939.[5] Umberto remembered him as a short, unpleasantly looking man, who followed his father into his parents' room and spent hours there speaking in whispers with him. Erminia Montini harshly chastised her husband for inviting this man to their house. Although Flor had officially joined the fascist party upon his return to Bolzano to avoid political persecution, she suspected he might still be under the watch of the secret police.[6] Her concerns, however, were incomprehensible to Umberto. According to his retrospective self-portrait, young Montini did not know what the difference between a communist and a fascist was—in fact, this seemed to him an irrelevant detail. Words such as

---

[5]Klara Rieder, *Silvio Flor: ein Südtiroler Kommunist im Einsatz für Arbeiter und Autonomie* (Bozen: Edition Raetia, 2007).
[6]Ibid., 63.

"*fuoriusciti*" (the political exiles of the fascist regime, around 300 of which lived in the Soviet Union at the dawn of the Second World War), socialism, and many other terms that he heard when he eavesdropped on his father's conversations with Flor were alien to Umberto. Nor did he know what his father's ideological position was because his old man never talked about it. His closeness to Flor made his father into an unlikely fascist, but Augusto never forbade Umberto to attend the pre-military courses or other fascist manifestations.

In a letter to Anfisa dated July 27, 1994, Umberto gave a slightly different version of his acquaintance with Flor. He wrote that he first met Flor during his last leave home before going to the Russian front, when his father secretly brought him to Flor's house. We cannot know which version is true. The story Umberto told in his memoirs might very well be a fiction in which the historical figure of Silvio Flor played a narrative function: it allowed Umberto to emphasize once again his lack of political consciousness, which in turn was the premise for his later political awakening. Both Umberto's acquaintance with Flor and his employment in a Jewish company were facts of his biography. However, they were also narrative devices, ways through which Umberto-the-narrator claimed he was not a true believer in Fascism, but just a young man whose lust for life compelled him to scorn ideology. "Politics?" Umberto wrote years later remembering his pre-Russia life, "I did not even know that there was a 'science' called 'political.'"[7]

At the same time, however, Umberto's political naiveté also betrayed his exposure to the fascist spirit that permeated Italy before the war. Since the 1920s, fascist thinking had promoted the idea that "politics" was a "dirty word, capable only of provoking divisions and arguments." As one historian has written, to avoid politics "had been one of the original motivating ideas of the fascist movement, even though, at some time, it had hidden a very active idea of intervention in the political life of the nation."[8] Thus, Umberto's conviction that his

---

[7] UM, "Descrizione."
[8] Paul Corner, *The Fascist Party and Popular Opinion in Mussolini's Italy* (Oxford: Oxford University Press, 2021), 66.

role was to obey, carrying out orders emanating from above rather than thinking about politics, might have been both part of his worldview at that time and a sentiment superimposed post-factum because it fit well with his story of political maturation and transformation.

From Civilian to Soldier

At 6 pm on June 10, 1940, Umberto joined hundreds of other Bolzano inhabitants on Piazza Walther to listen to the *duce*'s speech. In it, Benito Mussolini officially declared war on France and Great Britain. In Bolzano like in Rome, Milan, and other Italian cities, the crowds cheered to this war declaration with endless ovations.[9] Standing in the crammed square, Umberto hailed war, too, "perhaps even more than anybody else." He did so not only because he did not know what war was, as he wrote later in his recollections, but also because Mussolini's words made him feel "invulnerable."[10] They convinced him that Italy would win the war without much difficulty and that he belonged to the army that would conquer Europe. Vibrant with combative vigor, Umberto was animated with the impatient desire to fight.

The sobriety and misgivings of those few who did not share the general nationalist euphoria were incomprehensible to Umberto. Karl Bondy had given him permission to leave his desk "with neither enthusiasm nor censure," but, in Umberto's retelling of that day, it was the words of "Signor Otto" that most shocked him. Otto Bondy was the brother of Oskar, the company's founder, and himself a businessman involved in the company's running. As Umberto remembered, when he reentered the building after the crowd's bath on Piazza Walther, Otto was the first person he met. Having seen that Umberto was glowing with joy, the Jewish entrepreneur supposedly called him to the side and told him in a fatherly tone: "It's a pity for young people like you. We are getting into a dangerous adventure." Umberto replied that he did not understand, and Otto became more explicit. With a

---

[9] Some historians have questioned this spontaneity. See, Corner, *The Fascist Party.*
[10] UM, "Descrizione."

sad expression in his eyes and asking Umberto to keep the secret, he communicated to him his plan to leave for Valparaiso, Chile. "It is a pity that you are due for draft," added Otto, "otherwise you could have come with us."[11]

In fact, the encounter with Otto Bondy on June 10, 1940, could not possibly have happened because Otto and his family had left Bolzano for South America already on February 10, 1940. Umberto was by then not working at the Oskar Bondy anymore because the company was forced to close already on December 31, 1938, and the owner had been interned in a camp at Bassano del Grappa.[12] Clearly, Umberto made up this entire vignette. It was yet another authorial intervention through which he hoped to fashion himself as enthusiastic for war while also kind at heart and politically naïve. As he further commented in his recollections, he did worry about his employers but also wanted to be optimistic and convinced himself that their decision to go to Chile was most probably motivated by business reasons. Their advice to reduce his enthusiasm, their negative assessment of what was happening, and their prophecies about the coming of a bleak future sounded "unfounded" to him.[13]

It is easy then to imagine Umberto's jubilation when, around one and a half year later, on January 29, 1942, a post from the *Regio Esercito* called him to conscript service. The Bolzano military district headquarters was located on the same street where he lived. He got there early and quickly went through the intake medical examination, the first step in his transition from civilian to soldier. This was, in truth, a mild disappointment because the military doctor decided Umberto was unfit for the Alpini corps which he hoped to join. Twenty-year-old Umberto cut a tall and trim figure at 179 cm and 65 kilograms, a weight which, the doctor argued, would hardly bear the 40-kilogram backpacks usually carried by the Alpini. Instead, the doctor assigned him to the artillery corps and sent him to the Casale Monferrato

---

[11]Ibid.

[12]Innerhofer and Mayr, *Mörderische Heimat*, 284–5.

[13]UM, "Descrizione."

Figure 2.1 Umberto in January 1942.

barracks in Alessandria Province, Piedmont region.[14] Marching to the train station with the other draftees, Umberto walked by his home and saw his mother waving at him from the window. She must have rejoiced, Umberto thought, seeing how euphoric her son was.

The hard and monotonous life of the barracks, however, soon put a damper on Umberto's happiness and enthusiasm, while also challenging his fascist capacity for disciplined obedience to hierarchy. Upon arrival in Casale Monferrato, Umberto was put in a huge common room with bunk beds; he had no sheets to sleep in but only rough covers and a hard pillow; waking up in the morning, he did not see his beautiful Dolomites anymore, but only the lonely and far away peak of the Cervino Mountain. A simple corporal imparted orders and made the meaning of fascist military regimentation perfectly clear to all draftees since their very first day. There were constant military drills and, on top of everything, the food was ghastly. Soldiers were served meat soup and a loaf of tasteless bread at both lunch and supper. Initially, Umberto used the money he had brought with him

---

[14]AS, foglio matricolare.

from home to eat at least one meal a day at a restaurant in town. But when the money finished, Umberto was forced to eat the ration given in the barracks.[15]

Most unbearable of all for Umberto was the ugliness of his military uniform. The shoes were overly large, the sleeves of the jacket were too short, and the trousers should have been *alla cavallerizza* (jodhpurs), but in fact were something shapeless, in-between *cavallerizza* and *zuava* (knickerbockers). Refined Umberto, who had arrived at the barracks wearing an elegant white scarf over a brown coat and who until then had enjoyed outfitting himself for middle-class life, could not believe his eyes when he saw the image of his uniformed Self reflected in the glass door of the storage room. Soldiers were so poorly dressed that, he thought, they looked like "ridiculous scarecrows."[16] And yet, indifferent to Umberto's aesthetic sensibilities, the military officers made soldiers' ability to exit the barracks on leave conditional upon them wearing that uniform. Indeed, to enforce this rule, on their very first exit soldiers were ordered to go to the post office and mail their civilian clothes home.

Umberto had fortunately known about this rule already before arriving at Casale Monferrato and had come up with an ingenious plan to get around it. On the day of his arrival, before reporting to the barracks, he had wandered into town, befriended a young woman, and agreed with her that, instead of shipping his civilian clothes home, he would leave them with her and come to wear them every time he was off duty. The deal worked until somebody discovered his stratagem. On one of his off-duty days, Umberto had decided to go to the movies with a girlfriend (another one!). Wearing his civilian clothes but no hat, he entered the theater and sat next to an elegantly dressed couple. At a certain point, the man sitting by him touched his shoulder and said: "Artilleryman, immediately go and report to the sergeant on duty. I'll sort you out tomorrow." The man was the commanding officer of Umberto's battery and had recognized his draftee in the dark

---

[15]UM, "Descrizione."
[16]Ibid.

theater by his shaven head. For his act of defiance, Umberto got two days in the punishment cell (it was neither the first nor the last time this would happen) and was then ordered to mail his civilian clothes home and show the mailing receipt to that very commanding officer who had caught him. For a long time after that, Umberto did not leave the barracks on his off-duty days. He was ashamed of his ugly uniform and, since no "girl" would have even looked at him in that attire, he was no longer interested in going to town.[17]

Umberto's enthusiasm also waned because he saw a certain resignation in the faces of both his fellow soldiers and his superiors. The latter did not make any effort to keep the morale high among the draftees. The former had little clue about what was happening at the front or what would happen to them. There were rumors about mobilization and the training maneuvers that would have preceded it, but these were speculations that only left the young men disoriented. Some alleged that the Second Battery, to which Umberto belonged, would soon be sent to France or to Africa. Others mentioned Russia where, in July 1941, Italy had dispatched a 62,000-men-strong expeditionary force called the CSIR (*Corpo di Spedizione Italiano in Russia* or Italian Expeditionary Corps in Russia). When Umberto visited the young woman who was keeping his civilian clothes (before the incident with the commanding officer), he noticed resignation in her parents, too. Once, he overheard them whisper in Piedmont dialect: "Poor boys! They are so young. Where will they end up?" Those words seemed surprising and dangerous to a young man who had grown up surrounded by the cult of the *duce* and the fascist rhetoric of personal sacrifice in the name of the national cause. Not only had Mussolini repeatedly boasted throughout the 1930s of Italy's military strength, declaring that he could mobilize an army of "eight million bayonets," but in his speech on June 10, 1940, he had also bragged that the war was basically already won. Decades later, pondering on Fascism's military mismanagement, Umberto claimed that the issue was not shortage of resources but the fact that Italian weapons and equipment

---

[17]Ibid.

were not of the quality needed for a modern war: "yes, eight million bayonets, but they were tin bayonets." At that time, however, he could not understand why that Piedmontese couple talked about the war without the requisite enthusiasm. His own parents, in the letters they sent him every day, were more cautious but equally laconic. They did not include so much information as advice: "Be careful with this and with that. Do this. It's better not to do that. Remember that we are at war."[18] On his end, he sensed that something was going on which needed to be kept secret.

Then, one day, a group of recalled reservists arrived at the Casale Monferrato barracks. They were grown men from the classes of 1911 to 1919. Umberto became worried: weren't the young conscripts already enough to bring the army up to full strength? His curiosity pushed him to talk to the older reservists. Most of them were married and all of them cursed the war. Umberto could not hear the slightest enthusiasm in them. They did not even let him listen to the war bulletins: as soon as the news started, one of them would turn off the radio in anger. So, Umberto began to take refuge in the common room, where he drowned his emotions in bad wine and found distraction by writing letters on behalf of his many illiterate fellow soldiers. He had left home with so much joy and pride, but now he was becoming apathetic and disappointed.

After six months of this cheerless life, Umberto was granted a leave of forty-eight hours plus travel time. This was just enough time to make returning worthwhile, and Umberto took the opportunity to go back to Bolzano and see his family. There, however, the mood was sad too. Umberto's parents were consumed by the preoccupation for their son. One of his brothers told him that their father was secretly listening to Radio London: he would send everybody to bed, pull out a small device that Flor had given him, and listen to it covering his head with a blanket. Umberto had never heard of Radio London until then, but he guessed the dangerousness of what his father was doing and became very confused. Flor, who was still frequenting his parents'

---

[18]Ibid.

house, dropped by in the evening and advised Umberto to seek out a certain Guido Maršić, a 1917 reservist from Bolzano who used to work in the same print shop as his father and was now stationed at Casale Monferrato, too.[19] According to Flor, Maršić would be a good source of information against the surrounding fascist propaganda. This confused Umberto even more. How was he to understand the funeral-like atmosphere in people's houses and the advice Flor gave him when he still vividly remembered the great popular acclaim with which Mussolini's speech had been received on the crammed Piazza Walther?

Back at the barracks, Umberto found out that during his absence some of the batteries had been dispatched to Africa. He instead was sent to a tent camp in Giaveno, just outside Turin, where he joined a patrol of artillerymen called O.C. (*osservazione e collegamento*, or observation and communication). By the time Italy had entered the war, the basis of her army was a two-regiment *divisione binaria*, a structure whereby a divisional artillery acted as regimental batteries closely linked to the fighting infantry. Within it, the O.C. patrol was a team that specialized in the installation of artillery observatories and the set-up of communication lines between the collaborating artillery and infantry units.[20] As part of this patrol, in Giaveno Umberto resumed shooting exercises, now using cannons rather than shotguns only, but still with blank ammunition. The officers took great pains to explain that at the front ammunitions would have been real and the soldiers had to be ready for that. Umberto sometimes still imagined himself as a victorious warrior, yet he also feared that neither him nor any other recruit was ready. Guido Maršić, who Umberto in the end befriended as Flor had recommended, just repeated, "it's hard," and tried to put a break on Umberto galloping dreams of fame and glory. He also congratulated Umberto when they found out that his battery

---

[19]Umberto used two different spellings for this person's name: Marsick and Maršićick. I have opted for Maršić because Guido was of Slavic origin, according to Umberto's testimony, and Maršić is a common Croatian name.

[20]John Gooch, *Mussolini and His Generals: The Armed Forces and Fascist Foreign Policy, 1922–1940* (Cambridge: Cambridge University Press, 2007), 358.

was intended to go to France, a "luckier" location according to the reservist Maršić than the hot deserts of Africa or the frigid steppes of Russia. Chance, however, is quick to change, and Umberto was destined to experience its volatility first-hand.

One day, during marching drills, Umberto stopped to take a smoke. Having seen that, the drill sergeant called him out and began to read him a lecture, throwing all sorts of insults at him for failing to follow the rules. The insults did not touch Umberto until the sergeant pronounced one that concerned his mother. On hearing that, an inflamed Umberto stepped close to his superior and dealt a strong blow to his jaw. The sergeant fell to the ground; Umberto pounced on him and rained so many blows on him that blood began to come out his mouth. To hit a sergeant, regardless of how much the latter had abused his office, was a serious act of insubordination. Umberto was first escorted to the punishment cell and then to the commanding Colonel. The latter spoke briefly and harshly: "Instead of France, I'll send you to Russia. There, the cold will freeze your hot blood. Go away, you are a disgrace to the regiment." Of course, Umberto knew that arguing would have not helped, but he still had to have the last word. When he reached the door on his way out, he suddenly turned and blurted: "Colonel, I willingly go to Russia. We will win anyway. But please do not send that sergeant to Russia, too, unless you already want to put him in the casualties' list."[21] The escorting soldiers dragged him back to the punishment cell.

Thus, because of an act of indiscipline, the young fascist Umberto Montini was assigned to the ARMIR (*Armata Italiana in Russia*), an army of 229,000 men comprising seven infantry divisions and three Alpini divisions. With the help of these Italian units and additional Romanian and Hungarian armies, throughout the summer of 1942, the Wehrmacht had advanced deep into Soviet territory. By the Fall, this Axis coalition had reached the Don River's Soviet defensive line. It was there that Umberto would soon join it.

---

[21]UM, "Descrizione."

To the Front

When Umberto's entire battery was provided with new equipment and granted an extraordinary leave, everybody realized that departure to the front was imminent. It was perhaps for that reason that during his last visit to Bolzano Umberto was reluctant to talk about the war, but just tried to spend a few hours simply enjoying his family's company. He remembered that his mother looked at him as though she wanted to say something important, but all she could do was to smear his shoes with grease and provide him with advice about cold-related disease.

The only talkative person was the communist Flor, who, in the evening, came over to the Montinis house together with Guido Maršić. With everybody's eyes and ears on him, he said to Umberto:

Be careful. What the fascist propaganda says about Russia is not true. I was there. You should follow my advice. Winter is approaching. In Russia, winter is colder, much colder than here. Remember: when it will get colder ... and more snow will fall, that's when the Soviet troops will unleash a big offensive. Cover yourself well, especially your feet, and at the first occasion give yourself in as prisoners. The Russians will not treat you badly. They don't hate us Italians. But never stay with the Germans or even be close to them. The war will not last long. If you manage to give yourselves in as prisoners, the war will be over for you. You will not come back soon, but I repeat it to you, the Russians will not treat you badly.[22]

Nobody argued with Flor. Only Umberto protested: Wasn't this desertion? Wouldn't he be shot for this? But Flor seemed oblivious to his questions. Instead, he turned to Guido, asking him to stay close to Umberto and help him get rid of his militant nationalist dreams. As for Umberto's father, he did not say anything, but just stood up

---

[22]Ibid. See also AS, Umberto to Anfisa 27.7.1994. But in the letter Flor gave this advice to Umberto secretly, only in the presence of Umberto's father.

frequently and checked out of the windows to make sure nobody was surveilling them. On the following day, however, before going to work Augusto repeated to his son Flor's exhortations. "He is a communist," added the father, "the police keep an eye on him. He cannot listen to Radio London, but we do, and we tell him the news." Then the old man gave his son a hug and told him once more to always stay close to Guido. It pained Umberto to see his parents so worried and this time he left home with a heavy heart.

Going back to the barracks, he and Guido took a fast direct train to Verona, then a second one to Milan, and a last one to Casale Monferrato. They reported back to their officers with a ten-hour delay, in part because they had left Bolzano later than what they should and in part because they decided to hang out in Casale Monferrato instead of walking straight to the barracks from the train station. So, they were certain they would be thrown in the punishment cell for at least a few days, but instead, when they showed up at the gate and the guard checked their paperwork, they got only one night in the cell.

This and other changes in the barracks signaled to them that departure for the front would happen any time now. No drills were scheduled for those assigned to the O.C. patrol but only lectures and a sham hand-to-hand fight with bayonets. At night the trumpeter often sounded the alarm and the soldiers rushed into the barracks' yard in full combat gear. At times, the alarm sounded every hour of the night. In those nights, when sleep was constantly interrupted by the trumpet blast, Umberto's thoughts became even more confused and his spirits even lower. They were going to Russia, he thought, to advance and conquer, but at home people talked about surrendering. Flor said that the Russians were very strong and well prepared, that they were loaded with weapons, and had made a pact with General Winter. Entering Russia proud and rejoicing, the Italian army—Flor predicted in Umberto's narration—would have soon left it fugitive and miserable. Umberto wanted to talk about the confused thoughts that this prophecy generated in him, but Guido only smiled and repeated that he should just do as Flor had said.

Then, on a beautiful Fall morning, a warmer and less gloomy one than all the others there in Piedmont, they finally left.[23] Seeing the tractors, cannons, and machine guns, Umberto began to feel again like a warrior: the war that he had impatiently awaited had in the end arrived. The vehicles of the ammunition and food departments set out first, then the soldiers followed. Guido gave Umberto some pre-stamped military postcards and told him he should write "30th Corps Artillery Grouping" as the sender's address. Marching in a square with the officers in front of them, they arrived at the train station. There, they were greeted by a large crowd of young fascist women (*giovani italiane*) flinging flowers at them as was typical at soldiers' departures for the front.[24] Pretty and excited, the women cheered the soldiers as they went up on the wagons. Cigarettes, bottles of wine, and sweets, but above all hugs and kisses were freely exchanged. The military brass-band and the tricolor flags framed the entire scene as one of future triumph. During the trip to Milan, the soldiers drank wine from their water bottles, and in Milan more people acclaimed them with flags and brass-bands. In the crowd, Umberto saw the party secretary of the Milan section of the National Fascist Party, who was hugging the officers and greeting the soldiers with the Roman salute. Banners hung everywhere: "Win and we will win," "Believe, obey, fight." The same was seen in Verona with more brass-bands and more young women wearing the fascist uniform and singing fascist songs. They, too, gave the soldiers cigarettes, chocolate, wine, and cognac. On a troop train to Russia, the children of Fascism felt again the joy of war. "We will win!" wrote Guido Vettorazzo at the end of the letters he sent to Italy while crossing Germany and Poland.[25] "We were euphoric," concurred Umberto.[26] Yet, retrospectively remembering that train, he added that next to the jubilant young men and women were also some elderly people in tears, which brought Flor's apprehensive words back to his mind.

---

[23]It was October 16, 1942. Museo Storico Italiano della Guerra, uncatalogued Fondo Umberto Montini, "Dichiarazione integrativa" of the Italian Ministry of Defense.
[24]Sapori, *Marcher*, 133.
[25]Vettorazzo, *Cento Lettere*, 13.
[26]UM, "Descrizione."

* * *

Concluding Umberto's pre-Russia text, the descriptions of his last visit home, of the final preparations for departure to the front, and of the climatic train scene allowed Umberto-the-narrator to accomplish several goals. They gave him one last opportunity to contrast the omens of growing darkness with the exultation, trancelike state, and fever of victory induced in him and his mates by fascist propaganda. Crucially, by referring to Flor, these descriptions also helped Umberto prepare his readers for what would become apparent later in his narrative, namely the deceitfulness of Fascism and the strength of Soviet communism.

Aware of Umberto's authorial intent, we can also read both these specific episodes and his entire narration of his pre-war biography as historical evidence of how a young man might have felt in the late 1930s–early 1940s in fascist Italy. We clearly see not only Italy's increasing militarization and social mobilization but also the ways in which young people identified with these processes. Umberto drew the picture of an Italian people inebriated by patriotic fervor, enthusiastic about participation in the war, and mobilized behind its *duce*. At the same time, however, the mix of boldness and doubtfulness percolating Umberto's memory—albeit a signpost on a narrative arch—also reveals the extent to which obedience to hierarchy and war enthusiasm as the central tenets of fascist orthodoxy coexisted with less fascist feelings and behaviors, including reticence, reluctance, and a sense of resignation and dejection.

CHAPTER 3
THE "RUSSIAN FRONT"

In early December 1942, the Soviet Union launched the offensive "Operation Little Saturn," which aimed at entrapping the Axis force at Stalingrad and smashing those stationed on the lower Don. It was a wide-ranging strategy that involved breaking through the German, Italian, Hungarian, and Romanian winter defensive lines by means of armored forces, penetrating deep into the territory controlled by them and creating pockets of encircled units by going around them. According to official data released by the Historical Office of the Italian Army Staff, approximately 85,000 Italian servicemen (i.e., more than one-third of the ARMIR) died or went missing in that offensive.[1]

Among memoirists and historians, the Italian defeat and the military factors determining it have been the subject of many, sometimes sharply conflicting interpretations, ranging from the view that the Italian army's transportation means were inadequate to operate on the inhospitable terrain of the Soviet winter steppe to the depiction of poor equipment, clothing, and weaponry. Most of the around 200 memoirs published on the ARMIR nonetheless agree on defining its defeat as a "tragedy" and portraying the soldiers fighting in it as victims. Additionally, marking the anniversaries of the events in 1992–3, Italian state and public institutions made efforts to focus attention on the Alpini division "Tridentina" which, on January 26, 1943, broke through the Soviet encirclement at Nikolaevka. The Alpini's relative success represented an example that

---

[1] Ufficio Storico dello Stato Maggiore dell'Esercito italiano, *Le operazioni delle unità italiane al fronte russo 1941–1943*, 2ª ed. (Roma: USSME, 1993), 488.

Italians could be proud of and a more comfortable and heroic story to tell than the ARMIR's disastrous debacle.[2]

Umberto's writings about these events fit the Russian Text that I have mentioned in Chapter 1, offering a particularly raw and hallucinatory version of it. Far from including statistical data, overviews of economic and security situations, or analysis of military plans and diplomatic strategies, his memoirs and various notes were filled with the compulsive repetition of traumatic scenes that he relived through his senses. Vivid sensory (above all olfactory) details abounded in his text: "that dismal, flat landscape"; "that air poisoned by that acrid smell of smoke, burned gas, and death"; the "queasy smell" of blood; and the "disgusting smell of lubricant oil on hot weapons." Logic disappeared as Umberto described the days immediately preceding his capture and tried to convey something of the unutterable horror of retreat. He claimed that the soldiers had "liquified brains" and could not process what was happening: a sense of chaos prevailed over all other perceptions and capabilities.[3] Because of that, in remembering those days fifty years later, Umberto argued that he could recall only some seemingly trivial episodes, coming back to him in flashbacks of sights and sounds that scared him. Astray in the vastness of the Russian steppe and helpless in the face of both natural elements and human violence, he was focused on the minutiae of his environment and how his body moved (or lied) in it. Just like other soldiers telling their tales, Umberto described his terrible days in the strange places where he fought, but—at least at a first glance—he appeared as simply too traumatized to be concerned with events that happened outside his immediate field of vision and too overwhelmed to reflect on their causes and deeper meanings.[4]

At the same time, if we look more closely at Umberto's version of this Russian Text, we see that he did not simply connect the ritual of remembering the environment to the small-scale, confined-vision

---

[2]See "Selected Further Readings."

[3]UM, "Reminescenze."

[4]Hynes, *The Soldiers' Tale*. See also, Cathy Caruth, *Trauma: Explorations in Memory* (Baltimore: Johns Hopkins University Press, 1995).

process of his survival but also to how the larger-scale events of retreat and capture unfolded for the Italian and Soviet armies. His narrative was governed by raw bodily sensations, but it was precisely the embodied experience of being adrift on the "Russian front" that broke down the hopes of national triumph mobilized by Mussolini in him as well as in many other Italians. As other memoirists have described, when soldiers thought they had reached the limit of their moral and physical capacity to bear, they ceased imagining themselves as fascist victorious warriors and lost faith in the glory of war. The retreat constituted a decisive moment in the transformation story Umberto retrospectively narrated. And yet, his memory of it also had a clear experiential basis. It was a "deep memory," in historian Lawrence Langer's terms, that erupted from the caverns haunted by his physical distress and assaulted him, while also continually intersecting with his "common" or "reflective memory" to invest the incidents he recalled with meaning.[5]

Tormented by cold, haggard, and bereft of reason, in the Russian steppe Umberto not only gave up his identification with Fascism but also began to recognize the ineptitude of the ARMIR's Supreme Command. In fact, while seemingly deprived of discernment, his disjointed images still made clear the huge failures of intelligence and significant errors of judgment through which Italian leaders understood military realities on the ground. There was neither antifreeze in the Italian vehicles nor enough fuel, food, or indication of which path to go. The High Command did not take seriously the messages transmitted by its stronghold; it let precious days go by; and it issued the retreat order too late for the Italian withdrawal to happen in any disciplined manner. Thus, the events of December 1942 could

---

[5]Langer, *Holocaust Testimonies*, 9. Not only deep memory but also the other versions of memory that Langer identified in Holocaust survivors are useful to understand Umberto's memory of the Russian front as a "self-shattering event." Useful is also the approach that scholars of embodied history have taken to the memory of violent and traumatizing events in multiple fields, ranging from post-colonial studies [for instance, Antoinette Burton, *Archive Stories: Facts, Fictions, and the Writing of History*. Ed. Antoinette Burton (Durham, NC, & London: Duke University Press, 2005)] to the history of Stalinism [for instance, Natalia Kozlova, *Sovietskie liudi: Stseny iz istorii* (Moscow: Evropa, 2005)].

not possibly be a "fateful tragedy" as Umberto was concerned, but plain "criminal behavior."[6] Finally, as the Italian soldiers were captured and transferred to the POWs camps, Umberto's sense-driven narrative kept revealing mismanagements—this time of the Soviet army—and it was these inefficiencies—not Soviet taste for atrocity—that, in the final analysis, emerged as the root cause of the extreme violence surrounding him.

In this chapter, I focus on two distinct environments of Umberto's "Russian front": the town of Malevannyi and the steppe during retreat, capture, and march to the camps. By providing a thick reconstruction of how our memoirist remembered them, I explore the relationship between landscape, the body, and the memory of violence in a witness-survivor. Ultimately, this reconstruction shows that the *why* of violence was crucial in Umberto's memory journey and that body-centered recollections can teach us a great deal about the ways in which war (and trauma) survivors conceptualized the big historical events of which they were part.

Malevannyi

Umberto was part of the command unit of the 30th Army Corps Artillery Grouping led by Colonel Lorenzo Matiotti. Since November 2, 1942, this unit was stationed in the town of Malevannyi, just behind the Infantry Division Pasubio, which itself included the 79th and 80th Infantry Regiments and the 8th Artillery Regiment. Umberto served as German-language interpreter, responsible for translating communications between the Pasubio and the 298th Infantry Division of the Wehrmacht positioned to the Italians' left.[7] Whenever he received news from the German side, he wrote a report and delivered it to his unit's adjutant-major, Captain Itolli. This meant that Umberto enjoyed a privileged position that exempted him from

---

[6] UM, "Reminescenze"; and Museo Storico Italiano della Guerra, uncataloged Fondo Umberto Montini, "Chiarimenti e osservazioni."
[7] AS, foglio matricolare.

frontline service. Itolli was a strict officer, who gave orders with a sharp voice, always got straight to the point, and never apologized for anything, but he was also an exception among his peers in that he did not demand discipline in the same senseless and rigid manner as others did in the fascist army. With his fiery gaze, Itolli did not look down at his subordinates as worthless pawns, but rather strove to gain their esteem. While not counting him among his friends, Umberto nonetheless admired this officer for his courage and determination.

The town of Malevannyi was a small steppe hamlet around 200 kilometers to the West of Stalingrad. The few Russians who still lived there were all poor peasants. The unit's command had selected the largest and most solid-looking among their houses as its headquarters, while turning the hamlet's smaller *izbas* into makeshift barracks for the soldiers. This was a common practice for all Italian units in the area. Lodged in these peasant huts in groups of five or six, each serviceman had his own straw mattress and cover and, more importantly, a roof above their heads and a room where to take respite from the cold. Although it took some imagination for the Italians to define the Russian *izbas* as "homes," those housed there considered themselves lucky: in the *linea pezzi* (the cannon shooting line) both soldiers and officers slept in bunkers dug in the ground, "like in moles' lairs."[8]

Umberto's *izba* was right in front of the command's headquarters. Two women aged between thirty and forty lived there with their three young children in appalling poverty. Both women had lost their husbands during the war: one was declared deceased, the other missing in action. Remembering them decades later, Umberto stated that they had a "very beautiful relationship" with the Italian soldiers and that, despite the pain inflicted on them by the war, the two women took a liking to the Italians. This "sympathy" was certainly aided by the fact that Umberto gave them food. He secretly brought them bread and dry milk from the command's provisions. Sometimes, he also gave up for them part of his daily food ration, especially the vegetable broth that he greatly disliked. The children thanked him with a little rhyme of their own: "There is no bread and there is no corn // five people and

---

[8]UM, "Reminescenze."

there is no milk // but with the Italians we are good like in buttermilk." The women laughed when Umberto tried to speak Russian and used his hands to explain myself. They were mystified when he brought to their children some simple toys that he had especially asked his parents to send him from Italy through the Military Post. And they looked at him with curiosity when he melted frozen wine cubes, which he received as part of his ration, by placing them in his mess tin and burning coal under it.[9] In his published memoirs, *Cento Lettere dalla Russia* [One Hundred Letters from Russia], Guido Vettorrazzo, too, remembered both the indigency and the hospitality of the local population in the *kolkhoz* Pervomaiskoe. Like in Umberto's recollections, the village's women, "simple and gracious," looked favorably at the Italians and guided their attempts at learning Russian.[10] Both Montini and Vettorazzo (together with many other Italian memoirists) emphasized that the positive relations the Italians had with the locals distinguished them from other invaders and occupiers. Vettorazzo summed it up in a few words: "we were not the Germans."[11] This, Giorgio Scotoni has explained, was a standard "iconography of the 'Good Italians' in opposition to the 'Wicked Germans.'"[12] Meanwhile, the Russians were celebrated for their charity and humanity, a trope that continued to punctuate Umberto's memories as he narrated his capture and transfer to the place of internment.

A clear proof of the Italian soldiers' difference in handling the occupation was their approach to prisoners. Based on agreements between the German and Italian commands, Soviet soldiers captured by the Italians in the first year of the CSIR's campaign (July 1941–July 1942) were to be taken under Italian custody, provided with shelter and food, and then transferred to Romania from where the Germans would take them to Germany and put them to work. In fact, however, it was impossible for the CSIR to provide for the Soviet

---

[9]AS, Umberto to Anfisa, 18.5.1994.

[10]Vettorazzo, *Cento Lettere*, 54.

[11]Ibid., 56.

[12]Giorgio Scotoni, "Memoirs of the Russian Campaign and the new semantics of the Italian Soldier," *Nauchnye Vedomosti. Seriia istoriia. Politiologiia* 1 (2017): 161. See also Sapori, *Marcher*, 15–16.

prisoners because it lacked concentration camp facilities. As a result, the captives were usually first held in the Italian units' intelligence sections for questioning and then sent to camps under German surveillance. Later, when the CSIR was incorporated into the ARMIR in July 1942 and the Italians set up their own camps in the territories of the upper and mid Don, both armies managed Soviet POWs. Those in Italian hands enjoyed a gentler treatment than their mates captured by the Wehrmacht and were usually spared German brutality.[13] In Malevannyi, there were around twenty of these prisoners, mostly Slavic but some also from other Republics. In principle, Umberto remembered, they were to be transferred to the Italian Army Command in Millerovo. In practice, they were not subject to any strict surveillance. Once, for instance, a German officer came to Malevannyi with the intention to take away some Soviet prisoners. Irritated by the German's mixture of cockiness and contempt, Captain Itolli pointed his gun at him and, to his soldiers' acclaim, chased him away from the grouping's headquarters. After Umberto acquired the rank of *caporale* (corporal), he explicitly told the prisoners in Malevannyi that they could leave if they wished so. Yet, they preferred to stay: not only did they know that, according to Stalin's decree No. 270, soldiers fallen into enemy hands were considered traitors of the fatherland and subjected to harsh punishments, but many of them were indeed deserters.

Bored by the monotony of everyday life in "a barren desert" (as Umberto called Russia in a letter home from Malevannyi), he used every possible occasion to go to the prisoners' lodging and attempt to strike up conversations with them. This allowed him to practice his Russian and get to know the locals better. It was in this manner, for instance, that Umberto befriended Igor, a young man whose university studies had been interrupted by the war. With his help, Umberto learned several Russian words and began to conjugate some verbs correctly—not a small feat for any non-Russian speaker. If in Umberto's eyes the *izba* women represented "the typical Russian fatalism," Igor stood for the recklessness of the Russian youth, always

---

[13]Maria Teresa Giusti, *Stalin's Italian Prisoners of War* (New York: CEU Press, 2021), 37.

quick to shift "from the most unpredictable cheerfulness to the most teary fear."[14]

Besides translating communications to and from the Germans, in Malevannyi Umberto was also in charge of receiving messages from the Monastyrshchina stronghold, which was located halfway between his 30th Artillery Grouping and the Pasubio's first lines of defense. An old Kellogg field phone from the First World War and a less obsolete but equally malfunctioning field radio brought him the voices of the Monastyrshchina officers, Corporal Pierino Giudice and Corporal Major Luigi Balocco. Originally from Vercelli province, both men were cut from solid Piedmontese military cloth. Umberto happened to know them well as they had done their military service in the Casale Monferrato barracks and were later emplaced in the O.C. patrol. Precisely because he knew them well, Umberto could detect changes in their voices as the month of December progressed. First hesitantly, then with increasing determination, and finally with apprehension, Giudice and Balocco began to inform Commander Matiotti of the rattling noises that both their stronghold and the Pasubio's outposts heard every night. Assuming those were Soviet tanks, the two junior officers suggested they would soon be encircled and awaited orders and assistance from the Army Command. Indeed, since December 11, the Soviet army had begun to undertake a series of reconnaissance actions targeted at identifying the enemies' defensive position and obtaining tactical advantages over them in view of an upcoming offensive.

Fear, that "constant companion" of soldiers in all wars, began to wind through Umberto's grouping, too, as the signs increased of a possible Russian encirclement.[15] It was brought by some Italian soldiers coming from the Army Corps Command in Kantemirovka when they reported that they had seen Soviet troops just a few kilometers from Malevannyi. It also became palpable one night when some partisans entered Umberto's hut and removed the breechblocks from his and

---

[14]UM, Umberto's letter to uncle and aunt, 7.11.1942 and "Reminescenze."
[15]Martha Hanna, *Your Death Would Be Mine. Paul and Marie Pireaud in the Great War* (Cambridge, MA: Harvard University Press, 2006), 116.

his fellow soldiers' muskets. Although without harmful consequences, this action was a clear warning about their presence and ability to inflict damage. The officers became worried after this episode but kept going on with their business. The soldiers, on their end, were overtaken by a hectic and feverish mood, an unspoken anguish that nobody dared to voice aloud.

The incident that most impressed Umberto, however, was another one. One of the *izba*'s women approached him and began to talk to him in a maternal tone. Knowing that Umberto would understand at least part of what she wanted to tell him, the woman advised him to hide in her *izba*'s cellar. The Soviet troops, she explained, would arrive within three or four days; she would hand Umberto over to them and they would treat him well.

Astonishment and disbelief got hold of him. Still clinging to the illusion that the Italian guns and the artillerymen firing them were invincible, he brushed the woman aside with the argument that the Soviet army would never reach Malevannyi because "our guns" would fend off any attack. That was precisely what Mussolini had said in his December 2, 1942, speech to the Chamber of Fasci and Corporations.[16] Yet, doubts were increasingly crowding Umberto's mind. He had come to Malevannyi as the self-confident conqueror of a strange and unfamiliar land. But this town far away from the civilized and peaceful environs of his native Bolzano tested the limits of his military enthusiasm, and Mussolini's mantras, once exuding confidence, now sounded rather tentative to him.

Years later, Umberto wrote, "had I listened to that Russian woman, perhaps I would have saved myself that calvary." At that time, however, he saw two good reasons not to listen to her. First, Umberto supposed that Hitler's armored vanguard vehicles were just forty kilometers outside Moscow.[17] Had Malevannyi fallen to the Russians,

---

[16]Benito Mussolini, "Speech to the Chamber of Fasci and Corporations," December 2, 1942, http://www.ibiblio.org/pha/policy/1942/421202a.html. A few days later, the speech was broadcast by radio to the troops on the Russian front. See, Vettorazzo, *Cento Lettere*, 71.

[17]In reality, in November 1942, the Wehrmacht was 150 kilometers West of Moscow, on the Rzhev line.

it could be soon reconquered by the Germans. What then would be Umberto's fate? The Germans, he feared, would probably just shoot at him. Second, he was his grouping's interpreter: had he suddenly disappeared, his fellow soldiers would look for him. Instead of hiding in the *izba*'s cellar, Umberto went to the storehouse where the Italians kept the weapons they seized from the Soviet prisoners. From there he took a semiautomatic gun with a full cartridge and brought it back with him to the command unit. This action, which of course broke all rules of military discipline, was possible in those days because, as Umberto later wrote, "nobody checked on what we soldiers were doing."[18] Everybody was nervous as they saw sleighs passing by overloaded with wounded, dead, and frozen bodies. Without receiving any orders anymore, the Malevannyi soldiers were just waiting, unable to understand why so many frightened fellow servicemen were coming there from Millerovo.

Meanwhile, the telephone line between Malevannyi and Mostarsh-chyna was often interrupted by the increasing heavy bombardment coming from the Soviet artillery, until, one day (on December 17, according to a Russian memoirist) communications completely stopped.[19] For a few hours, the phone operators could not connect with the Italian stronghold there, and then, suddenly, they intercepted a call. On the other side, however, the familiar voices of Giudice and Balocco had disappeared to be replaced by an unknown German soldier who was trying to communicate with the 298th German Division. Quickly, the operators called Umberto to act as interpreter, but by the time he got to the phone, the soldier's voice had become very weak and all he could hear through his sobs was *"hier sind alle tod"* (everybody is dead here).[20]

---

[18]UM, "Reminescenze" and "17-18-19 dicembre 1942."

[19]Sergei Ivanovich Filonenko, *Ot Pruta i Dnestra do Dona i Volgi: razgrom armii satellitov fashistskoi Germani pod Stalingradom i Voronezhem* (noiab. 1942 g.-fevr. 1943 g.) (Voronezh: Izdatel'stvo VGU, 1999).

[20]Giudice was last heard on December 12, 1942. He was then declared missing in action. Balocco, instead, died during imprisonment in a Soviet camp on February 25, 1943. UM, letter of the Vercelli Military District, 28.5.1993.

Retreat

Cold, hunger, thirst, and fear were the overpowering sensory and emotional background upon which the "apocalyptic days" of retreat, capture, transfer to the hospital unfolded for Umberto.[21] These harrowing bodily sensations marked his experience—and every single memory he later recalled—of his "Russian front," an environment that in Umberto's mind stood apart from both Malevanny and Zubova.

For his grouping the official retreat order arrived on December 20. It was minus 30 outside and so cold that the oil in the lorries' engines had frozen and the vehicles did not start.[22] Spouting blasphemies, the drivers burned hay under the engines to help them come back to life. Colonel Matiotti and the other officers had gathered all the topographic maps, compasses, and orientation devices available in the camp and then settled on two *giardinetta* (station wagon) cars with canvas roofs. The Colonel had summoned Umberto and ordered him to "stay by his side at all times" so that he could be his personal interpreter in communicating with the withdrawing German units. Through him, Matiotti asked for information, consulted German maps, and talked with the German officers who crossed their path.

Initially, Umberto kept calm. He did notice that Matiotti was more worried than usual, but he still considered retreat as a normal part of the Italian army's military tactics. Only as retreat turned into rout did he, too, become alarmed. Lorries flanked the officers' cars and swiftly went ahead of them, but nobody knew in which direction they were moving. Still, even more powerful than fear on that first day of retreat was hunger. Nobody seemed to have thought about loading food supplies on the officers' cars and, having consumed his only ration, Umberto became very conscious of this lack of food.

It was hunger above all that pushed him to take an impromptu decision. As Matiotti's *giardinetta* was overtaken by another lorry, Umberto heard his name called out by the driver. He turned and, to his

---

[21] UM, "Reminescenze."

[22] Italian motor vehicles were not provided with anti-freeze. Giusti, *Stalin's Italian Prisoners*, 14.

surprise, saw his friend Guido Maršić at the wheel of a tractor carrying shapes of grana cheese and boxes of crackers (typical provisions for the Italian troops in the Second World War). In a split second, Umberto jumped off the command car, boarded Guido's vehicle, and began to use his bayonet to carve out pieces of cheese. While he stuffed his mouth, he heard Matiotti order him back. But, besides food, there were ice cubes of wine on Guido's juddering tractor and Umberto did not budge. As it turned out, the bravado by which Umberto joined Guido (attracted as he was by the cheese, crackers, and wine) was a fateful one. A few days thereafter, Matiotti's *giardinetta* broke through the Soviet encirclement by guessing a "hole" in it and, after two months on the road, brought all its passengers safely back to Italy. At that time, however, Umberto could not know about this. He just rejoiced when he saw the Colonel's car disappear behind a small hill: that meant that Matiotti would never punish him for his indiscipline.

When the tractor stopped because it ran out of gas, Umberto and the other soldiers on it realized that they were in serious trouble. By then bedlam had exploded: columns of Italian, Romanian, and German soldiers had formed spontaneously, their members walking aimlessly in all directions. "Infected by despair," he and his companions left the tractor without taking anything along: "neither a cracker, nor a piece of cheese, or a can of meat."[23] None of them had a compass either. The tide of desperate people engulfed Umberto's small group and each of them began to walk next to strangers. Whenever Umberto passed by a German, he asked for news, but nobody wanted to speak as all focused on saving their energies.

Soon, fear became so strong that it acted like a narcotic making Umberto forget the aching in his body. He did not know what he looked like but assumed he was just like all the other soldiers around him: wearing tattered uniforms and bruised faces, indescribably dirty, with long beards infested by lice, their young features hardened by anguish. Over their shoulders or in their hands, they carried their muskets; in their haversack, they had their Balilla hand grenades: the

---

[23]UM, "17-18-19 dicembre 1942."

soldiers sought safety in these weapons, but they were almost useless now. Realizing that, Umberto threw away both the semiautomatic gun he had taken from the storehouse and his pouches with cartridges and hand grenades. After a while, he also disposed of his backpack in the attempt to walk more quickly, yet still arduously slithering forth and back in the untrodden snow.

The withdrawing soldiers, Umberto wrote, found themselves "cynically abandoned … to a fate that anybody would try to spare to even the most disgusting and vile animal." Overtaken by the ever-growing despair and acting by instinct, they began to disperse. The officers seemed resigned to defeat, too: they ripped off their ranks from their uniforms and threw them in the snow. Together with fascist party cards, badges of various types, and miniature *fasces lictoris* (the Roman rods and shield symbol that represented fascist authority), now the ranks lay over the white expanse around Malevannyi and extinguished any hope of rescue the soldiers might still have. The "murderous steppe," as Umberto called it, was also studded with bundles of rags containing the lifeless bodies of his fellow soldiers. Very few still had their helmets on (the soldiers had learned that these were good only as conductors of cold), but balaclavas and other types of coverings hid their faces, leaving only the eyes exposed to the unforgiving cold. The soldiers' mouths were covered, too, as it was dangerous to take full breaths of frozen air. Some of them looked like they were sleeping, while others had eyes wide open, and Umberto thought that "death had streaked [their eyes] with terror and horror." At night, when the steppe's wind buffeted them by lifting ice dust, cold itself turned into a cynical killer, "an invisible, lethal, and sadistic enemy," bestowing death to the retreating soldiers. Umberto saw many wounded men curl up without complaining and just wait to fall eternally asleep, anticipating the liberation that death would bring them. At the "glacial" temperature of the Russian steppe in December, Umberto explained to a potential editor in one of his notes, freezing felt like a numb sensation, a paradoxically bearable, albeit merciless and lethal aching that slowly took over the entire body and brought soldiers to death almost without pain. For those who walked by them, however, those bodies lying in the landscape like frozen stones marked a path of agony and desperation.[24]

"War," in the words of historian and Second World War veteran Samuel Hynes, "turns landscape into anti-landscape, and everything in that landscape into grotesque, broken, useless rubbish—including human limbs." In this anti-landscape, the first sight of the dead dramatizes war's "strangeness" and "unfamiliarity" for civilian soldiers.[25] Like other enlisted men before him, when Umberto saw the first corpses, he felt his anguish increase, but he kept moving, "blind, albeit with eyes wide open, desensitized, cold as the ice upon which he stepped."[26] The corpses slowly became part of his "anti-landscape"—no longer just a physical space punctuated by remnants of a catastrophe but rather a sad nightmare and a haunting vision that would persecute him for many years to come.

Along with the sight of corpses, the pangs of hunger vividly dramatize the disruption of normal life in Umberto's retrospective writings. He remembered that soldiers would eat anything and, having turned into "monsters," would "kill a brother for a crust of bread."[27] Once, for instance, he found a group of Romanians butchering a dead horse and fighting over its innards. Afraid to even get close to them, he picked up the horse's excrement and began to eat it greedily until his friend Guido approached him and shared with him a tiny frozen chicken.

Amidst the retreat's brutality, Guido's act of kindness stuck indelibly in Umberto's memory. Yet, this is a problematic recollection for us. How could Guido get that chicken? We know that the food dropped by the German aircrafts that circled above the retreating soldiers included only dry items. Did Guido steal it from an *izba*? And does it even matter where the chicken came from or whether Guido could truly produce it and share it? Indeed, the entire figure of Guido Maršić is enshrined in mystery. From the *giardinetta* episode onward, Guido systematically

---

[24]UM, "Reminescenze," commenti 30.1.1994, and note dated January 1999.
[25]Hynes, *The Soldiers' Tale*, 8 and 67.
[26]UM, commenti, 30.10.1993.
[27]UM, "17-18-19 dicembre 1942."

popped up in the darkest moments of Umberto's narration, his image tightly intertwining with flashbacks of brutality. In line with scholars of memory, one might say that Umberto remembered Guido through "common memory," that is the memory that reassured him that some human bonds could never be violated.[28]

What happened a couple of days after the retreat had started is another example of these intersecting memories of unredeemable atrocity and remaining humanity. Umberto had decided to follow a small group of soldiers including Italians, Germans, Romanians, Hungarians, and a few Spaniards and Finns, all heading South-West in the hope to meet the German army moving toward Stalingrad. The sky was so clear that night that they could see the North Star, yet the cold was so unbearable that their bare fingers would get glued to the metal at touch. Observing the Soviet tracer bullets, around ten of them attempted to organize a strategic offensive to break the encirclement. Umberto grabbed a gun and a hand grenade from a corpse's haversack and started to move with the others out of the riverbed where they were hiding. On his way to certain death, however, Umberto found Guido, who ran after him, delivered two sound slaps to his face, threw him to the ground, and hurled away his weapons. Once again, Guido appeared in Umberto's narration as a character that supported him and ensured his survival. His memory had "nurturing value" and provided comfort whenever Umberto's "deep memory" excavated the most unsettling incidents of his war experience.[29]

Capture

It was hard for the retreating soldiers to see the Soviets and impossible to know whether those surrounding them were regular units of the Red Army or partisans acting autonomously. Their numbers were unclear too: there could be one hundred of them or up to three or four thousands. Regardless, they were everywhere, sowing an increasing

---

[28]Langer, *Holocaust Testimonies*, 9.
[29]Ibid.

sense of panic among the defeated troops. Furthermore, besides the Red Army and the partisans, there was a third enemy encircling the retreating Italian army and laying traps for them: the *fuoriusciti*. Many of these Italian communist exiles to the Soviet Union had joined the Red Army, where they were assigned the special task of dressing up as junior officers of the Italian Army, infiltrate the mass of the scared, drifting soldiers, and, pretending to lead them out of the encirclement, send them straight to the Soviets. It was hard for the Italian soldiers to recognize their own officers in the bedlam of retreat, and these new ones spoke perfect Italian. Paradoxically, their service to the country that had welcomed them and saved them from fascist persecution was also a determinant factor in saving Umberto's life since it was thanks to a *fuoriuscito* that he and other dispersed Italians ended up captured by the Soviet Army instead of dead in the frozen steppe.

After the failed attempt at breaking the Soviet encirclement, Umberto's group was reduced to around fifteen soldiers. Continuing to move South-West, one day they saw an Italian lorry drive by them. It was empty, with only the driver at its wheel. When it stopped, they all boarded it and began to move to a site where the Soviets were firing with more intensity. At a certain point, the driver said the Soviets had seen the lorry and asked everybody to jump off and get away from that easy target. Umberto thus recounted what happened afterward:

> Together, silent, with eyes wide open, we lay down in the snow … An artillery or mortar discharge hit our small group. As common in those cases … one could hear the others pray. Even the atheists prayed, all prayed and invoked one person only – their *mamma*. It is difficult to remember how it happened. I only know that when the artillery fire ceased, I tried to shake the comrade next to me. He did not move; warm, coagulating blood spilled from his neck; his head was almost detached. Shocked, I stood up, began to touch my body, to check if I still had two legs and two arms. I was deaf. A pitiless and criminal deafness had taken hold of me. I headed toward the lorry, turning at times

to see if somebody from our group followed me. Nobody. They were all over there, either dead or wounded.[30]

Umberto could not remember for how long he stood petrified by the lorry. Neither could he recall what exactly was happening around him. He just saw himself looking at the dead and wounded comrades he had left behind and being unable to move until a man wearing the ranks of sergeant major punched him in the face, screamed "What are you waiting for, cretin?," and dragged him to the lorry.[31] A new driver started the engine and headed off in yet another unclear direction. After a few hours, the car stopped again, and again it became the target of Soviet artillery attack.

Realizing that any type of resistance would be in vain, the Italians decided to surrender. A soldier hoisted a white rag on his bayonet and this action, "like a charm," made the firing stop.[32] The same sergeant who had hit Umberto to shake him out of his shock now ordered all the soldiers to toss down their weapons: a pile of guns and hand grenades quickly built up by the lorry. Without waiting too long, the Italians heard agitated voices speak in Russian to them. Of course, most of them could not understand what was being said but they instinctively raised their hands and climbed down the lorry. Umberto, instead, stayed behind: he wanted to see whether the Soviets would kill the prisoners on the spot. Only when he ascertained that no shots were fired did he leave the vehicle.

A Soviet soldier with an ugly and cruel, pockmarked face walked up to Umberto. Calling him *fashist* and *bandit* and pointing his automatic gun straight at his stomach, the soldier began searching him. He snatched Umberto's watch, his chain with the image of the Madonna, and his wallet; he took out the money the latter contained and then threw the rest away onto the ground. At that, photographs of Umberto's brothers, ex-girlfriends, and beloved mother spread out on the snow—he never got them back. Then, the soldier resumed

---

[30]UM, "17-18-19 dicembre 1942."
[31]Ibid.
[32]Ibid.

frisking Umberto's body, looking for any weapon the Italian prisoner might have hidden. Although Umberto believed he had thrown away all arms and had reassured his captor that this was the case, the Soviet soldier found a Balilla hand grenade on him which had by chance slipped out of the haversack and nested between the lining and the fur of his overcoat. Pulling out the grenade, the Soviet shoved it under Umberto's nose, meanwhile pushing the barrel of his gun even harder against his stomach and screaming all sorts of insults at him. Umberto saw death coming at him.

> I fixed the gaze on my mother's photograph and waited for that grim Russian to pull the trigger. He instead looked at me. Ordered me to turn. I thought he did not have the courage to shoot me in the face. I turned and no longer saw my mother's photograph. Terrible instants. I observed an endless column of prisoners which was walking on the top of a small hill and which I thought I would never join.[33]

But instead of shooting him, the Soviet soldier kicked him hard in the back and ordered him to run up to the other prisoners, a column of Germans, Romanians, Italians, and Hungarians silently marching in the snow.

That was the night between December 24 and 25, 1942. Umberto was reminded it was Christmas by the sad voices with which a group of Germans sang *Stille Nacht* as if it were a lament rather than a Christmas song. "Always methodic and precise," wrote Umberto years later, the Germans did not neglect tradition even in that situation.[34] Still more strikingly, unlike soldiers from other nationalities, they held on to the certainty that one of their Panzer divisions was on its way to save them. That division, however, never arrived, and the singing Germans were captured or killed while defending their vain hopes. That day Umberto promised himself that, if he survived, he would never celebrate Christmas again.

---

[33]Ibid.
[34]Ibid.

The *davai* March

In Italian memorialist literature, the transfers of prisoners from the sites of capture at the front to various labor camps and hospitals in the interior have become known as "the *davai* marches"—by the Russian word *davai*, which the Soviet soldiers shouted at the marching prisoners to keep them moving and which translates into English as "come on" or "forward." In fact, the transfers were not only marches: they usually started by foot under the Red Army's surveillance and ended by railway under the NKVD's supervision. In both phases, they were characterized by logistical incompetence caused by lack of preparation, proper means, manpower, and competent directives.[35] Umberto described them as "inhumane, endless, and deadly" for all but the strongest. He also claimed that these death marches killed more prisoners than the labor camps in which the survivors were placed. At the same time, while denouncing "the macroscopic inefficiency" with which the transfers were carried out, Umberto also identified an important extenuating circumstance to their disastrous character: since the goal of the Soviet army's offensive unleashed against the German and Italian divisions on the Don was not to capture them but rather to create confusion and force the enemy to back off, the Soviets had not foreseen the need to deal with such high numbers of prisoners. Historians have shown that, against Umberto's opinion, operation Little Saturn was aimed at "liquidating" the Italians.[36] Our memoirist's falsification should, once again, be understood as part of his authorial intent to depict the Red Army in a positive light. Accordingly, he also asserted that the extreme violence caused by mismanagement turned the Soviets into victims too.[37]

For Umberto, the "exhausting calvary of the march" lasted approximately seven days.[38] During that time, he covered around

---

[35]Sapori, *Marcher*, 216–19; Giusti, *Stalin's Italian Prisoners*, 45–52. Decrees to improve prisoners' transfers began to be issued in the fall of 1943. Zolotarev and Emelin, *Russkii arkhiv*, 117–25.

[36]Scotoni, *L'Armata Rossa*, 201.

[37]Centro di archiviazione RAI BOLZANO, teca T92359/051; AS, Umberto to Anfisa, 18.5.1994; and UM "17-18-19 dicembre 1942"; and "Sorvolando."

[38]UM, "Sorvolando."

300 kilometers, all by foot and in arduous environmental conditions, provided only with threadbare and unsuitable equipment, and surviving on scarce, inadequate food rations. Looking at the distance from the top of small hills, all he could see while marching was barrenness, blizzards, and dark silhouettes slowly moving in the pitiless landscape. Above him was an immense, leaden, and sad sky. At times, airplanes crossed it, but Umberto and the other soldiers did not care to understand to which army they belonged. Resigned to their fate and trying to save energy, the prisoners avoided talking during the day. At dusk, when their column stopped for the night, they lay next to each other to keep themselves warm and fell asleep on the ice. Not all were able to stand up in the morning. Those who did were increasingly tormented by hunger and thirst.

On the second day of march, the prisoners walked through a cluster of *izbas*. Some women hurriedly came out of them, left at their entrances buckets filled with water, and quickly went back in. Breaking out of the column, the thirsty prisoners threw themselves on those buckets, while the guards shot in the air and screamed at them to get back and keep walking. In the confusion, Umberto sneaked into one of the peasant huts. As he entered, the stench of boiled cabbage, mold, wet clothes, and sweat hit his nostrils. He saw two women and an old man with a long white beard. He also saw icons in a corner and, invoking *"Khristos"* and crossing himself, he begged for something to eat. In response, the old man stretched out a hand with something dark and solid in it: it was a piece of hard bread made from sunflower seeds. Umberto thanked them for their piety and quickly exited the *izba*. Once outside, however, a group of prisoners assaulted him to take the food out of his hands. Umberto fell on the snow and was left with only a tiny piece of bread clenched in his closed fist, which he devoured immediately. The rest was reduced to small crumbs and became a bounty over which the crazed prisoners fought, hitting each other with the little strength that was still in them.

The remaining days of the march looked all the same. The long, dark strip of desperate prisoners trudged with difficulty in the immense white expanse of snow. Umberto found himself walking by an increasing number of corpses, which, like in the retreat, lay curled up in a frozen, eternal sleep. In his memoirs, he defined them as men who had failed the test of courage as endurance and decided to let themselves die.[39] Other corpses, albeit less, lay spread out a few meters away from the beaten path: they belonged to prisoners who had attempted to run away and were shot by the guards. A few prisoners also died during the sudden attacks inflicted upon the column by irregular troops riding on horses. We do not know who these men were. Some prisoners thought they were Don Cossacks. Rejecting this guess, Umberto speculated that these "demoniac, crazy individuals" were partisans who acted "out of control" and "were perhaps drunk."[40] Two or three times, they flanked the column and discharged their automatic weapons on the prisoners. Their bodies were left where they fell: abandoned and unburied.

Once, looking at these lifeless bodies, Umberto felt envy, and the lure of giving in to death grew strong in him. He threw himself to the side of the beaten path and waited for the cold to take his life. Umberto would have remained there forever if he had not been saved by his loyal friend Guido, who, having seen Umberto lying in the snow, quickly lifted his body and forced him to reopen his eyes. Guido's words, "*ancora uno sforzo*" (one more effort), became the mantra that since that day the two friends repeated to each other as they kept moving with the rest of the column.[41]

If the sight of his fellow soldiers' corpses had been so depressing as to inspire Umberto's gesture of suicidal despair, the view of those still alive and walking was equally miserable: they wore tattered clothes and frozen balaclavas (often stolen from their fallen comrades), icicles covered their long beards, a myriad lice sucked blood from their dirty bodies, and their bowed heads and sagging gait made them look like drunkards about to fall. In fact, their clumsy way of walking was

---

[39]On soldiers' suicide as failing the "test of stoic courage" see Hynes, *The Soldiers' Tale*, 59.

[40]UM, commenti, 8.3.1994. Other survivors remembered that "the worst behavior toward prisoners came from partisans … and from members of the cavalry." Giusti, *Stalin's Italian Prisoners*, 43.

[41]UM, commenti, 18.8.1994.

determined by their footwear. When the feet are frozen and tired because of prolonged standing, they swell. Shoes and boots then cause sharp pain. It was because of these conditions that, apart from a few Germans who still wore their boots, most prisoners had cut through the leather of their suddenly small shoes, taken them off, and wrapped their feet in sheepskin rags ripped from their overcoats and held together with their puttees. Wearing such "shoes"—some as large as 30 or 40 centimeters—the prisoners were forced to drag rather than flex their feet, which ultimately made their steps more stable but also awkward. Some had also tied hay around their legs to help against rheumatic pains, but Umberto could not say if this solution helped against the cold, too.

As for the Soviet soldiers supervising the convoy, unlike other memoirists, Umberto remembers them in a relatively positive light. Although their incessant "*davai, davai*" still haunted him in his nightmares, he also claimed that,

> we did not see them as sinister jailers and, honestly, we did not hate them. Perhaps, they hated us (and for good reason) ... but they did not show it by giving vent to excessively strict behaviors or vindictive instincts ... Certainly, I saw raw episodes, but not acts of true, premeditated, and gratuitous violence.[42]

The guards cursed and insulted the prisoners; they spit in their faces, threatened them, violently shoved them. Instead of distributing the available cabbage and potato broth to the prisoners, they simply poured the watery slop onto the snow and let their captives lick it. And when the POWs drew water from the occasional wells they came across, the guards pressed them with shouts and blows of their rifle butts to quickly move on. However, Umberto insisted, the Soviet soldiers were neither tormentors nor executioners. There was no indiscriminate, random, and unmotivated shooting during the march to the camps, but only the cold killing of those "suicidal" prisoners who abandoned the column and tried to run away. Like the prisoners,

---

[42]UM, commenti, 8.3.1994.

the guards suffered from hunger, and they, too, squabbled over the distribution of pieces of old bread. Instead of trigger-easy evil doers, Umberto thus presented the guards as aware of the inhumanity of the march, burdened by the duty to obey blindly, and even "unhappy to see all those dying people"—in a word: not ferocious beasts, but resigned and human.[43]

After a week of this excruciating march, the miserable caravan arrived at its destination—a railway junction where other columns of prisoners had gathered and where all the captives were pushed into the cattle wagons of a long train. There were twenty of these wagons, each containing around 100 prisoners crammed up one against the other. There was no room in them to sit down and no way to shift one's body position. In the stampede of Soviet soldiers nervously shouting orders, firing their guns in the air, and shoving bodies onto the train, Umberto lost sight of his friend Guido and never found him again.[44] Later, in the memoirs, Guido's disappearance became the last of a series of events that dramatized the narrator's loss of any sense of normality. Indeed, left without his "guardian angel," during the cargo train transfer Umberto felt his mental health completely deteriorate.[45]

* * *

While centered in the body and its most basic needs, Umberto's reckoning with the "Russian front" also delivered more than just his sensory perceptions. Remembering his survival in the frozen steppe, Umberto confronted both the harrowing sensations of cold, hunger, and fear *and* the unpalatable truth that victory had eluded him, retreat had turned into an unmitigated disaster, and his country

---

[43]Ibid.

[44]Ibid. Guido was never repatriated. Speculating on what happened to his friend, Umberto formulated the hypothesis that he was taken to the Temnikov labor camp and, at the end of the war, decided to stay in the Soviet Union following his communist sympathies.

[45]I have analyzed Umberto's self-diagnosis of "madness" in my paper "'I am a war wreck': Mental Health, Self-Diagnosis, and Political Reckoning in the Life-Writings of an Italian POW in the Soviet Union," presented at the conference "Against the Norm: Disability in Eastern Slavic Literature, Film, and Culture" (Paris, Universite La Sorbonne, June 20–21, 2024).

had "murderously sacrificed" its soldiers.[46] All his senses worked together to evoke feelings and sensations of past events, while also providing routes to his attempts to both navigate and explain the loss of normality caused by those events. Indeed, the very description of bodily sensations and emotional states was part of a healing process because it helped reconstructing memories and bringing back normality. Thus, while Umberto's close-perception position generated a collection of fragments, it was precisely through these fragments that the surviving, traumatized witness made sense of the violence that shattered his Self in broader historical terms.[47]

Umberto's "Russian front" ended at Zubova Poliana. Since July 1941, this town in the Autonomous Republic of Mordovia had been the location of a military hospital which, under the management of evacuated health personnel, had first treated injured Soviet soldiers and then, after March 1943, the prisoners of various enemy armies. It was one of the 178 "special hospitals" (*spetsgospitali*) created by the Soviet authorities to detain captured POWs, and it became the destination of the around 150 men on Umberto's train who were injured and sick. Those who still preserved some health, instead, remained locked in the train and were transported to various labor camps along the Pot'ma-Temnikov railway line.[48] Later, as the Red Army advanced West in 1943–4 and took more prisoners, new arrivals kept coming to Zubova. These included also the Soviet soldiers of General Vlasov's collaborationist Russian Liberation Army who had

---

[46]UM, "Reminescenze."

[47]Langer, *Holocaust Testimonies*; and Judith Herman, *Trauma and Recovery: The Aftermath of Violence—from Domestic Abuse to Political Terror*. New York: Basic Books, 1992. Svenja Goltermann defines "memory fragments" as "spontaneous and abrupt statements" that emerge from a traumatized soldier's "chain of associations." Svenja Goltermann, *War in Their Minds: German War Veterans and Their Experiences of Violence in the Second World War* (Ann Arbor: University of Michigan Press, 2017), 307, footnote 56.

[48]"Archival note" from the Central Archive of the Ministry of Defense of the Russian Federation, http://www.zubova-poliana.narod.ru/warheros1-hospital2.htm; Adol'f Afanas'evich Prokhorov and Gennadii Nikolaevich Petelin, *Zubova Poliana* (Saransk: Mordovskoe Knizhnoe Izdatel'stvo, 1998), 71; and Zolotarev and Emelin, *Russkii arkhiv*, 7.

been captured and handed over by the Allies after the German defeat. Accused of betrayal, these soldiers were first treated at Zubova and then sent to Temnikov for forced labor.[49]

By the time Umberto arrived there, he was so hungry, cold, and fatigued that he briefly passed out when his wagon's door opened and the guards pushed the prisoners to climb down. When he came back to his senses, he found himself first lying in the snow next to the railway and then being barreled into the hospital by two Soviet women.[50] All around him resounded an uproar of orders, moans, screams, and machine gun discharges. Drifting in and out of consciousness, as he remembered decades later, he could also hear how the two women tried to console him: "You are not dead," they said, "you are just very sick, but you will recover and soon go back to Italy. The war will be over, and we Russians have won! Do not worry."[51] They were right: Umberto would recover and go back to his country, yet not before spending three full years interned in the Zubova Poliana hospital.

---

[49] Anfisa witnessed the arrival at this convoy of prisoners in May 1945. UM, Anfisa to Umberto, 13.3.1995.

[50] One of the hospital attendants, Liubov' Trofimovna Kharitonova, remembers dragging half-dead prisoners out of the wagons, putting them on sleds, and taking them to the hospital. "Pochti vse nashi vrachi zarazhalis' ot ranennykh tifom i boleli …" http://www.zubova-poliana.narod.ru/warheros1-hospital4.htm

[51] UM, "17-18-19 dicembre 1942."

CHAPTER 4
INTERNMENT AT ZUBOVA POLIANA

In the camps and hospitals managed by the NKVD, some prisoners could secure more favorable conditions than others thanks to their skills, the kind of work they performed, their willingness to act as informers, and other ameliorating factors. Umberto had a certain degree of freedom at Zubova. His role as interpreter enabled him to entertain a friendly (perhaps collaborating) relation with the political commissar Sergei, while his liaison with Polina expanded his access to information and medical care. At a first glance, he seemed to have adapted well to captivity. However, Umberto's pressing thoughts about the "contradictions" of Soviet life and especially the "serious illness" that he contracted toward the end of his internment betrayed the limits of his adaptation. Desiring to pay his "debt of gratitude" to "Russia" for having saved his life, when he wrote his memoirs, he retrospectively described his psychological ailments at Zubova as deriving from an "unjustified" depression. But at the time he was a prisoner, they were a clear indication that, far from being just a site of salvation, the POWs' hospital had also been a place of confinement where his war traumas had lingered and deepened.

For an historian, the concerns, salient events, foodstuffs, and interactions Umberto recalled having with his captors and fellow prisoners are all significant memories because they provide precious glimpses into the normality of daily life in a Soviet POW hospital. Without forgetting the narrative intentionality of Umberto's memoirs, in this chapter I draw on the concept of the "exceptional normal" and suggest that, since Umberto was an "outlier" in comparison with many other survivors of Soviet imprisonment, he had "a peripheral gaze" on the taken-for-granted horrors of captivity.[1] What appears exceptional about him might have been normal in terms of how internment unfolded for other POWs, too.

Special Hospital No. 1631

The Zubova Poliana hospital complex (*spetsgospital'* no. 1631) included four departments spread over a territory surrounded by two rows of barbed wire and surveilled by armed guards standing on watch towers. Wards 1 and 2 were in a former school building on one side of the railway line. In them, incoming POWs were treated by a team of four surgeons—two Soviets, whose names remain unknown, and two Italians named Luigi Filippi and Mario Landi, themselves POWs. Wards 3 and 4 had been set up in Zubova's old pedagogical gymnasium on the other side of the railway. No. 4 was devoted to the isolation and treatment of prisoners who had contracted tuberculosis or some other infectious disease, but only a few left it alive.[2] This "death's antechamber" was headed by Doctor Anna Ivanovna Tarasova, a middle-aged, petite woman with a melodious voice and a kind heart whom the Italian prisoners had nicknamed "mammina." Ward 3, instead, was a convalescent department hosting those who recovered from tuberculosis or needed post-surgery treatment. Directing it was Doctor Pavlina (Pelageia in the passport) Evteevna Ovodkova. Younger than Tarasova, Ovodkova was similarly known among the prisoners for her professional competence and compassion in treating all prisoners equally, regardless of their nationality. Both Soviet doctors appeared to their Italian colleagues Landi and Filippi as "missionaries," performing their job without adequate equipment and material resources.[3] Like other wartime and Gulag doctors whose

---

[1] Laura Almagor, Haakon A. Ikonomou and Gunvor Simonsen, eds., *Global Biographies: Lived History as Method* (Manchester: Manchester University Press, 2022), 12–13.

[2] "Gospital' dlia vonennoplennykh v Zubovoi Poliane," http://www.zubova-poliana.narod.ru/warheros1-hospital1.htm

[3] UM, "Osservazioni," and commenti 28.3.1994.

Figure 4.1 Mario Landi (undated).

biographies have been recently recovered, Tarasova and Ovodkova attempted as much as they could to improve prisoners' lives within the constrained milieu of the POWs' hospital.[4]

Since Umberto had arrived at the hospital with frostbitten legs, he was first treated in one of the surgical wards. He could not recall whether this was no. 1 or no. 2, but he clearly remembered how it looked. On the ground floor was a huge, horseshoe-shaped room, in the middle of which stood a stove big enough to heat the entire space. Along the walls hung a two-level scaffolding of wooden boards that served as beds. The prisoners lying on them were myriad, and they all looked dismal. Most of them wore a shirt or a thin blanket provided by their Soviet captors, but some were completely naked

[4]Alexopoulos, *Illness*; and Dan Healey, *The Gulag Doctors: Life, Death, and Medicine in Stalin's Labour Camps* (New Haven, CT: Yale University Press, 2024).

because their old clothes had been removed for disinfection and not replaced with new ones. Their heads and genitals had been shaved to get rid of the lice that infested them, but, as it turned out, these parasites never completely left their bodies. Without any muscle left in them, the prisoners were skin and bones, skeletons lying directly on the rough boards. Very few were able (and willing) to stand up and climb down the scaffolding to go to the bathroom, which was really just a big hole with two parallel boards by its sides separated from the room only by a makeshift division of four slabs nailed together. The smell coming from that filthy pit mixed with that of the prisoners' gangrenous flesh and starkly polluted the air in the room. Fifty years later, when Umberto thought about his first days at Zubova, he could still smell the stench of this ward, see the prisoners' sunken faces, and hear their moans and prayers all around him.

1942–3 were the worst years of the war, when the already meager resources available in the Soviet camps and military hospitals became even more strained and when conditions such as the inadequate disposal of feces further spread disease and all sorts of epidemics.[5] While many died in the "purgatory-like" conditions of wards no. 1 and no. 2, Umberto survived because he had the "good fortune" to contract tuberculosis and be moved to Doctor Tarasova's care in ward no. 4.[6] Without having access to streptomycin (an antibiotic which began to be used in late 1944 in the United States), this woman cured her patients only with rest and the administration of calcium chloride and vitamin C through IV injections.[7] In Umberto's case, the treatment miraculously worked. It also helped, Doctor Landi thought, that a spontaneous collapse occurred in Umberto's left lung, which caused a condition of "localized rest" to the area affected by the pulmonary disease and ultimately increased his chances at healing.[8] After five

---

[5] Alexopoulos, *Illness*.

[6] UM, commenti, 11.4.1994.

[7] Mary Schaeffer Conroy, *Medicines for the Soviet Masses during World War II* (Lanham & Plymouth: University Press of America, 2008).

[8] This, at least, was the thinking of contemporary doctors. See, for instance, Ross K. Childerhose, "Pneumothorax treatment of tuberculosis. A clinical and roentgenological evaluation," *Radiology* 27, no. 6 (December 1936): 741–8.

months in ward no. 4, in early summer 1943, Tarasova considered him healthy enough to go to the convalescent ward. Umberto spent the next three years of his life there, slowly adapting to the conditions of captivity and allowing his everyday life to acquire some normality.

Adaptation and "Normality"

Once beyond the immediate danger of death and safely settled in ward no. 3, a crucial factor in Umberto's process of adaptation was his encounter with Doctor Ovodkova, or "my Polina" as he called her. When they first met, Umberto was struck by "her youthful face, kind gaze, silken voice, and indestructible smile which made light of any dramatic situation." About her Umberto also came to appreciate the fact that she was humble, shy, kind, and thoughtful. She talked neither about herself nor about politics, but just completely devoted her energy to her mission as a physician. Polina, as Umberto remembers her, was a "doctor-angel" who never abused her authority in the hospital, was never angry, felt genuinely sorry about the scarcity and inadequacy of the medicines available to the prisoners, was upset every time one of them died, and, most importantly, cured not only the physical but also the moral condition of all her patients. Thanks to her "humaneness," "spiritual help," and the "comfort" she especially gave to Umberto, he became able to tolerate his "depression." The nightmares that haunted his sleep in the first months of internment slowly disappeared. He realized that he could still be useful to somebody and have reasons to live on. As he later wrote in a letter to Polina's children, "I was born twice. Doctor Pelageia Evteevna gave me a second life in 1943."[9]

Other POWs, too, entertained romantic liaisons with Zubova's women. For instance, a Polish prisoner named Janko (captured when he served in the German army as a forcibly inducted soldier) became the lover of a nurse working in ward no. 3. Able to write in Cyrillic,

---

[9]UM, commenti 28.3.1994 and 30.7.1993, Umberto to Bortolin 12.4.1993, undated note to Polina's children; AS, Umberto to Anfisa 20.9.1993 and 18.5.1994.

Figure 4.2 Polina in 1945.

Janko used to send love messages to this nurse. One day, however, the commissar got hold of a note and, soon thereafter, both the nurse and Janko disappeared. We might guess they were tried by a military court and perhaps sent to labor camps. Even more tragic was the love story between prisoner Marino Appolloni, originally from Rome, and a nurse called Shura, a brunette who did blood and spit analysis in ward no. 3. When Shura saw that Marino's Koch bacillus test had come back positive, she secretly passed on this information to her lover. They knew that this test result meant Marino had tuberculosis and would be moved to ward no. 4. Because they did not want to be separated, they decided to falsify the test results. This stratagem, however, quickly led to his death. "To die for love is something marvelous!" wrote Umberto in a letter to Anfisa.[10] Yet, it was not exactly "love" that killed Marino. Knowing that his chances of recovering in the "death antechamber"

---

[10]UM, commenti 5.7.1993; AS, Umberto to Anfisa 14.3.1994.

Figure 4.3 Marino Appolloni in May 1942 before leaving for the front.

were slim anyway, this prisoner probably just desired to spend the last days of his life next to somebody who cared for him.

In his recollections, Umberto clarified that most relationships between POWs and local women were neither so intense nor so catastrophic as Marino's and Janko's ones. "It was not rare," he wrote, "that the nurses stopped by the Italians' room in the evenings ... I remember a prisoner from Milan [Danilo Seveso], a real joker, who embarrassed me with his requests to translate risqué comments to various nurses, yet his were just responses to the equally risqué questions he received [from the women]." Of course, to make sexual innuendos, show excessive familiarity, and sing love songs to the nurses trespassed, the rules of captivity and the expectations placed on Soviet women concerning relations with foreigners. Yet, this trespassing was a routine occurrence because the realities on the ground made it nearly impossible to limit interactions and those charged with preventing them could be lenient. For instance, although the head nurses had the task to check on the behavior of their subordinates, including their relations with prisoners, they themselves "were far from behaving like jailers."[11] On his end, the political commissar Sergei suspected that the Italian prisoners might fall in love with the nurses and often threatened to intervene, but, as far as Umberto could remember, he meted out punishment only in the case of Janko, when he had undisputable proof of an ongoing relationship.

Historian Raffael Scheck has argued that, despite strict prohibitions, harsh punishments, and public shaming, uprooted prisoners far away from home and war-weary women "facing a shortage of local men in their age bracket" often fell in love with each other during the Second World War. As Scheck discusses in his study of "forbidden relations" between Western POWs and German women, postwar memoirs, fiction, and historical publications either glossed over these liaisons because they contradicted the image of the POWs as "heroic or stoic victims" or portrayed them as "conquest[s] making up for the defeat … and the symbolic emasculation of the captured soldiers." However, Scheck explains, the motivations for these relations were much more "contradictory and ambivalent" than how they have been represented in postwar culture. Furthermore, although "most couples did not think very much about the political implications of their actions," their personal relations were ultimately political acts challenging wartime policies and rhetoric designed to inspire hate of the enemy.[12]

Umberto did not play up any Italian patriotism which, in principle, should have prevented his fellow prisoners from engaging in love affairs with the local population. To the contrary, he recognized that both the hospital's captives and the Soviet women played an active role in flirting and seeking sexual contact or just affection. When it came to his relationship with Polina, however, Umberto completely

---

[11]UM, commenti 11.4.1994.

[12]Raffael Scheck, *Love between Enemies: Western Prisoners of War and German Women in World War II* (Cambridge: Cambridge University Press, 2021), 1–5.

de-sexualized it, rather framing it in terms of "compassion" and "humanity." This is especially evident in his Italian writings. We have no description in Umberto's memoirs of their courtship and the first steps they took in developing their relationship. The former POW only recounted that the two of them spent many "happy hours" in Polina's office, where he taught her the German language and she reciprocated by helping him improve his Russian, and where he helped her file patients' clinical records—both activities being great excuses for enjoying contact. In his Russian letters to Anfisa, Umberto recalled more details of the special bond that tied him to Polina. For instance, he mentioned that once, on the day of his birthday Polina secretly gave him an entire pack of cigarettes as a gift. In another letter, he declared that, after discovering what had happened to Polina after the war, he "envied" the man who had become her husband. He also confessed his obsession for Vittorio De Sica's 1970 film *I Girasoli* [The Sunflowers], in which an Italian soldier missing in action in Russia is saved by a local woman whom he marries. Once, Umberto explicitly revealed to Anfisa "the secret" of his "feeling" for Polina, yet immediately asked his correspondent to keep this confession to herself and reassured her that in the hospital he had "suffocated" this feeling. As Umberto insisted, theirs had remained a platonic love: "true, pure, and beautiful albeit brief and without the usual happy ending." Anfisa, too, remembered Umberto's and Polina's special relationship in similarly de-sexualized—but slightly more allusive—terms. She wrote, "you were with her all the time. I remember your lessons in the duty room, behind the curtain, where Polina Evteevna had her office. We all, the nurses and I, were always there and … we heard everything. Personally, I always respected these lessons."[13]

Although we cannot know the extent to which Umberto acted upon his feelings or "suffocated" them—perhaps fearing the political commissar might punish him for them—the fact remains that both he and Anfisa represent his relationship with Polina in very different terms from those they use to remember the unions between other

---

[13]AS, Umberto to Anfisa, 18.5.1994, 29.6.1994, and 12.4.1994; UM, commenti 11.4.1994, and Anfisa to Umberto, 28.3.1994.

prisoners and nurses. Why? What pushed them both to sublimate it into feelings of gratitude to an "angel"?[14]

I do not believe that Umberto avoided discussing the sexual nature of his relationship with Polina because of the humiliating quality it had as a non-fully consensual one. Yes, Polina had both unhindered access to his body and the power to excuse him from heavy outdoors physical labor. We know from other memoirs that Italian prisoners would gladly give up their tobacco rations in exchange for being recognized sick by the camps' female doctors.[15] We cannot thus exclude that Umberto was likely to please her anyway he could because she was his "ticket[] to survival."[16] Nonetheless, nowhere in his writings did I see evidence that their bond was degrading for him. More likely, modesty and reservedness played a role here. Umberto's recollections were intended for a public audience, and Anfisa knew that Umberto read her letters together with his wife Licia. Thus, both wanted to avoid representing Polina's involvement with him in any way that could be morally judged as unprofessional and lecherous behavior. Even more crucially, their understanding of the political meaning of Polina's feelings compelled them to practice some self-censorship in describing this aspect of Umberto's life at Zubova. Personal relations with any POW constituted a serious crime under Soviet law because they reversed the propaganda of hatred for all invading enemies. In addition, intimate connections with foreign prisoners upended wartime myths of national solidarity and representations of Soviet wives and girlfriends as eternally faithful to their men. Because loyalty to the men at the front was a moral obligation and a patriotic responsibility, entertaining a relationship with a foreigner was deplorable. Writing fifty years after the war, Umberto and Anfisa were unlikely worried about the legal consequences of Polina's behavior (who, by the time, was already dead). But they both appeared eager to

---

[14]Wienand has seen this retrospective transmutation of sexual desire into feelings of gratitude for their "saving angels" also in the memoirs of some German POWs. Yet, she has offered no analytical explanation for it. Wienand, *Returning Memories*, 168.

[15]Nuto Revelli, *La Strada del Davai* (Einaudi: Torino, 1966), 13.

[16]Alexopoulos, *Illness*, 92.

preserve nationalist and gendered Soviet myths. They did speak openly about the love affairs of other nurses and prisoners. However, because in their writings Polina was not just a Soviet doctor but often stood for "Russia" itself, Umberto and Anfisa wanted to protect her memory from any story that would impugn her integrity and associate her with treasonous "collaborations of the heart."[17] Polina's loyalty could not possibly be represented as divided: she had to be a "doctor-angel," performing her duty as healer of individual patients notwithstanding the fact that they were enemies and enhancing Umberto's life thanks to her professional talents and human traits. Her Hippocratic ideals (unlike any potential romantic feelings for Umberto) were not in opposition to her patriotism.[18] Through this portrayal, our memoirist upheld a representation of Zubova as a place of lasting value, while simultaneously prohibiting himself from dealing with aspects of his emotional life which were integral to his internment.

Alongside Polina's "comfort," key in how Umberto settled into "an alternative reality during captivity" was also his recruitment as the ward's interpreter—and perhaps informing collaborator.[19] When he was moved to ward no. 3, he first assisted Marino Appolloni in performing translating duties and then stepped into his position when he died. At that point, Umberto was tasked with two official responsibilities: 1. to translate the political commissar's and the commanding sergeant's communications to the prisoners; and 2. to form teams of prisoner-workers and assign them to services for which the Soviet doctors and nurses had required extra assistance, such as carrying the laundry to the washhouse or fetching water from a nearby stream.[20] Since these teams were multinational, it was the translator's

---

[17]Raffael Scheck, "Collaboration of the heart: The forbidden love affairs of French prisoners of war and German women in Nazi Germany," *The Journal of Modern History* 90, no. 2 (2018): 351–82.

[18]For a discussion of Soviet doctors' loyalties and their place in local histories of Gulag towns, see Healey, *Gulag Doctors*.

[19]Scheck, *Love between Enemies*, 20.

[20]This was in line with decree no. 335 on the utilization of convalescent POWs' labor. Zolotarev and Emelin, *Russkii arkhiv*, 103.

job to explain what they had to do and then follow them outside the fenced camp to communicate any additional requests to them.

Unofficially, the political commissar also demanded Umberto's daily visits to his office to learn about the prisoners' "political orientation" and whether they had complaints or were organizing any escape plan. Young, confident, smart, argumentative, and always suspicious, this NKVD officer was Zubova's main political authority.[21] In his memoirs, Umberto claimed that he sometimes interceded with the commissar Sergei on behalf of other prisoners and often had "lively," "dogged" discussions with him. Yet, Umberto was always confident that Sergei would not take any serious disciplinary measure against him because he was the only one who knew most of the languages spoken in the camp (Russian, German, Italian, and Romanian).[22]

The special treatment that his "friend" the commissar reserved to Umberto should be interpreted more critically than what our memoirist claims. In the camps, tasks such as commanding and managing other prisoners were entrusted to those who responded well to Soviet propaganda and demonstrated some ideological growth from the perspective of their Soviet captors.[23] Most probably, the NKVD officer had noticed that Umberto displayed interest toward communism and strove to create a special bond with him in the hope to control the talks they had. For instance, the questions he asked Umberto about Italy were not simply the starters of polite conversations, but excuses to give him lessons about the fallacies of Western capitalism as opposed to Soviet communism. When the commissar encouraged Umberto to attend a local school for a few months, his goal was to let Umberto have enough understanding of written Russian so that he could read Marxist literature. Finally, although a man with such impressive linguistic skills was definitely useful, the commissar must have also made sure to keep checks on Umberto (perhaps even through Polina!) and to test the extent of Umberto's potential for "conversion" to communism. One day, for example, the commissar came up with

---

[21]Two other commissars assist him in his duties, but Umberto barely interacted with them.
[22]UM, commenti, 7.5.1993 and 2.7.1993.
[23]Giusti, *Stalin's Italian Prisoners.*

a proposal that seemed surprising to Umberto but in fact was part of standard techniques of Soviet political re-education (and that other Italian POWs had accepted in other camps).[24] He asked Umberto if he desired to enroll in the antifascist school of the Krasnogorsk camp, in the periphery of Moscow, where foreigners were taught Marxism-Leninism and offered Soviet citizenship. Without squarely rejecting the idea, Umberto bode his time waiting to see how the war would end. As he put it later, "what would happen if I accepted and then the advancing Germans captured me?"[25] Regardless of Umberto's vacillation, what matters here is that Zubova's political commissar could have applied any number of coercive methods to subjugate the Italian prisoner, but he had no intention in distancing himself from Umberto. On the contrary, Sergei wanted to gain Umberto's trust and possibly Sovietize him. On his end, Umberto tried as much as possible to navigate this relationship to his own advantage.

Thus, while the position of interpreter was not always comfortable, it was certainly a privileged one. Umberto had multiple bosses, needed to translate their orders to a vast number of prisoners, and was under pressure to keep them working. He was vulnerable because, at any time, he could displease any of his bosses or reveal too much about his fellow soldiers. But this job exempted him from any physically demanding labor, gave him significant decisional power, and made him valuable to many people in the camp, ranging from the sergeant commanding the guards to the nurses, the doctors, and the prisoners themselves. Umberto knew he was a prisoner whose favor was coveted.[26]

The Hospital's Information Landscape and the POWs' Social World

An important component of internees' daily life in Soviet camps and hospitals was their access to information, including their exposure

---

[24]Giusti, "Dal fascismo al communism"; and *Stalin's Italian Prisoners*, 146–52.
[25]Umberto quoted in Ferrandi, "La', in Russia."
[26]See, for instance, UM, commenti 7.5.1993.

to political re-education and the "crisis of values" it engendered.[27] At Zubova, political indoctrination was carried out mainly through the distribution of brochures printed in the POWs' national languages. *Freies Deutschland* [Free Germany] was the German-language bulletin and *Romania Libera* [Free Romania] the Romanian one. Their Italian counterpart was the journal *L'Alba* [The Dawn], which was edited by the Italian communist leader Palmiro Togliatti under the pseudonym Ercoli. Furthermore, the hospital—like many other Soviet POW camps—was visited by Italian *fuoriusciti*, who made efforts to spread their communist views. Finally, there was an elderly officer who read aloud news about the war from the journal *Pravda*, with Umberto translating in Italian, German, and Romanian. These group readings provided prisoners with very little knowledge about the course of the war on any other front than the Soviet one. Both *Pravda* and the brochures in the prisoners' languages barely mentioned the Allied landings in Europe or the Allied economic cooperation with the USSR and, when they did, they strongly de-emphasized these actions' role in the conflict's progress.[28] The hospital workers, for their part, were wary of unguarded speech and answered the prisoners' question about the war and their future repatriation as though they were reciting lessons learned by heart.

Under these conditions, most prisoners ended up doubting the truthfulness of the information they received.[29] Some responded to Soviet propaganda with fatalism and resignation. Doctor Filippi, for instance, shrouded himself in an absolute silence, refusing to pronounce any assessment on either the Soviet people or the prisoners' chances to go back one day to Italy. When he left for the front, his wife was pregnant and at Zubova he could only talk about her and his dream to have a daughter. Others, like Doctor Landi, turned everything into a joke and pretended to be always cheerful, yet theirs was a mask

---

[27] Giusti, *Stalin's Italian Prisoners*, 155.

[28] Olga Kucherenko, "Lend-Lease in War and Russian Memory," in *The Memory of the Second World War in Soviet and Post-Soviet Russia*, 155–79.

[29] See also Melchiorre Piazza, "50 anni fa … per loro la fine di ogni speranza," *Il Notiziario U.N.I.R.R.* 13, no. 49 (January–March 1996): 1–2.

behind which lay a deep pessimism. Indeed, Umberto wrote, the hospital's lingering "atmosphere of secrecy, surveillance, and mystery" bred a "constant psychosomatic crisis" in many prisoners. Ailments as banal as food poisoning would become life-threatening to them, and they would sometimes look at death as liberation. Some prisoners let themselves die of starvation, while others walked up to the barbed wired to provoke the sentinels to kill them. All were taken by a great sadness as they looked out of the hospital's windows, saw nothing else than snow, and feared they would never be repatriated.[30]

Within this politically loaded information landscape and amidst the scarcity of verifiable knowledge available to prisoners, Umberto's position was—once again—quite peculiar. His official role as the hospital's interpreter, his unofficial alignment with the commissar Sergei, and his closeness to Polina made him able to observe behaviors and hear information that remained invisible and unheard to most others. This, however, did not always lead to less emotional pain or better understanding of the hospital's reality.

Some of the information that Umberto uniquely possessed was just factual. For example, although the political commissar was adamant that the prisoners should not know the name of the town and the region where they were kept, Umberto managed to find that out. This happened by chance one day when, escorted by the hospital guards, he walked by the train station and, practicing his newly acquired skills in reading the Cyrillic alphabet, he deciphered the name "Zubova Poliana" written on the building's facade. Another day, he overheard a nurse apostrophize a colleague as "dirty Mordovian" in the heat of an argument. When Umberto asked the insulted woman what "Mordovian" meant, he quickly discovered that this was the name of the region where he now lived as a POW. To the political commissar's chagrin, Umberto also knew about the existence of labor camps along the Pot'ma-Temnikov railway line, not far away from their hospital.

Other pieces of information were more distressful to Umberto. He was horrified, for instance, when he learned about the autopsies that a female surgeon performed on the corpses of those prisoners who

---

[30]UM, commenti 5.7.1993, 7.5.1993, and 30.7.1993; "Ho tutte le ragioni."

had died from undiagnosed ailments. "How could I exclude," Umberto wrote in his memoirs, "that sooner or later I, too, might be opened up by her implacable scalpel?"[31] In other words, in the context of captivity, the medical procedure of forensic examination by a pathologist—which was "routine" in the camp hospitals—felt to Umberto like an omen of his own death.[32] Equally painful to him was the knowledge he once acquired about deceased prisoners' burials. The job to dig pits in the woods outside the fenced camp, fill them with corpses, and then cover them back with soil was assigned directly by Sergeant Repkin to the hospital's "fritzes" (as the German prisoners were called), although at times the Italians Danilo Seveso and Lino Cellenza were involved, too. Each pit contained between ten and fifteen corpses, all of different nationalities and all completely naked. After the diggers finished their macabre task, the Soviet guards planted a pole on the pits with a number embossed in fire on it. This number was then marked in the upper right corner of the deceased prisoners' files, thus allowing to know in which common pit each of them was buried. While this procedure was kept secret from other POWs, Umberto was told about it by Polina as he helped her bind these files and pack them in boxes for shipment to the political commissar's office. Instead of giving him solace, this extra information deeply pained him because it made him realize that individual soldiers' remnants would forever remain impossible to identify.[33]

Finally, because of his role as interpreter, Umberto was able to develop a bird's eye view on the social world of the POWs' hospital, which included prisoners of several nationalities: not only Italians, Germans, Romanians, and Hungarians, but also a few Czechs and Poles as well as one Spaniard and one Austrian. His comments and comparisons of the prisoners' national characters deserve some discussion. First, they show how carefully Umberto avoided defining the POWs solely as the Soviets' victims. This, of course, was in line with his authorial intent to deconstruct ideas of Soviet brutality. Second, his

---

[31]UM, commenti, 14.5.1994 and 16.10.1993; and AS, Umberto to Anfisa, 16-28.1.1994.

[32]Alexopoulos, *Illness*, 90; and Healey, *Gulag Doctors*, 180–200.

[33]The prisoners' "cemetery" was impossible to locate later because the poles had been removed and the funeral mounds had been leveled with the ground. See UM, Anfisa to Umberto, 26.8.1994.

comments indicate the extent to which the racialized interpretations and psychological vocabularies of the 1930s had worked themselves into his understanding of the hospital's inhabitants. Like those of other surviving witnesses, his "positive or negative experiences as POW[] were mixed with preexisting racial and nationalist prejudices."[34]

According to Umberto's national typologies, the Italians, Romanians, and Hungarians tended to be "apathetic towards anything." Especially the Hungarians looked "impassible, as though wearing a wax mask on their faces." The Germans, instead, seemed unable to accept defeat and, with their perceived arrogance, inspired resentment in the Italian POWs. The Germans' "unbroken optimism" and their "deeply rooted feeling of superiority" as well as the Italians' antipathy for them punctuate the accounts of other memoirists, too.[35] But Umberto, it must be noted, had a specific reason to emphasize the difference between the Germans and the Italians: since he was from *Alto Adige* (South Tyrol) and came from a mixed Italo-Austrian family, he was eager to distinguish himself from those German-speaking or bi-lingual *altoatesini* (South Tyroleans) who in 1939 had opted for German citizenship and gone to serve in the Wehrmacht. Thus, he argued that already during the march to the hospital the Germans' gazes had been grimmer than those of the other prisoners; their souls (which, Umberto thought, "were made of the same metal as their guns") filled with greater rancor and contempt. At Zubova, Umberto averred, the German POWs initially upheld their cockiness, their conviction of racial superiority, and their anger at having been captured. "Whenever possible they sabotaged the work [they were assigned]" and variously refused to execute orders. Slowly, however, even the proudest among them realized that the Soviet guards were not to be joked with; they became meeker and conformed to life as POWs, all the while still keeping a certain distance from the other prisoners and silently despising them. The German prisoners' fighting

---

[34]Wienand, *Returning Memories*, 167.

[35]Hilger, "Re-educating the German Prisoners of War: Aims, Methods, Results and Memory in East and West Germany," in *Prisoners of War, Prisoners of Peace: Captivity, Homecoming and Memory in World War II*, ed. B. Moore and B. Hately-Broad (Bloomsbury Publishing, 2005), 61–75, quotation at 61 and 74. See also Sapori, *Marcher*, 71–5.

spirit sharply declined in 1944–5, when Nazi soldiers as young as seventeen and as old as fifty-five began to flood the hospital. These were captured members of the so-called *Volkssturm*, the citizen army of young teenagers and old men called on to defend the beleaguered Reich in the Fall of 1944. The news of German defeat that the new captives brought with them weakened the morale of other fellow German prisoners.[36]

After the Germans, the second most significant national group at Zubova were the Romanians. Thanks to his knowledge of Latin, which he had studied in school for seven years, Umberto quickly picked up their language and easily conversed with them. In his memoirs, he often wrote about the "huge" differences between the Germans and the Romanians: the former "stubborn, fanatic, snooty, but loyal"; the latter duplicitous, incoherent, "sneaky, too pliable," and sometimes slightly "schizophrenic." As opposed to the Italians, who, in Umberto's eyes, represented a united group both in political and in ethnic terms, the Romanians were divided. Not only did they belong to multiple national groups which could not stand each other, but they also displayed a variety of views on both the Antonescu government and Nazi Germany, which led them to sharply argue with each other. Umberto was often forced to scream and curse at the Romanians in the morning assembly when he assigned daily jobs to the hospital's prisoners: only by seeing him angry, he claimed, would the "inherently lazy" Romanians follow the orders he translated.[37]

Worst of all among the Romanians was, in Umberto's racist view, the "gypsy" Ignat, "a specialized and hardened thief, a lazy bone, and a liar," whose only value in the camp was his special gift for thieving without ever being caught. Once, Umberto recalled, Ignat managed to steal some bread from Repkin, while another time he stole a razor from a nurse. At the time of repatriation in the Fall of 1945, Ignat did not know where to go. Thus, he proposed Umberto to accompany him to Italy and set up there a common business that would have quickly made them both very rich: to steal and re-sell. As Umberto

---

[36]UM, commenti, 7.5.1993, 16.10.1993, and 8.3.1994.
[37]UM, commenti 16.10.1993, 5.7.1993, and 13.2.1994.

put it jokingly, "[Ignat] would have conjugated the first verb, and I the second."[38]

Less despicable but equally insufferable to Umberto was the Romanian Dobrota, "a religious maniac," who had many icons by his bed and, burning his portion of butter as though it were a candle, prayed over them. Once, "rendered crazy" by his faith, Dobrota attempted to run away from the camp to go to Moscow and meet Patriarch Alexius I, the head of the Moscow Patriarchate that Stalin had just re-established after decades of official persecution. Dressed up as a woman, Dobrota managed to sneak by Sergeant Repkin's surveillance, leave the hospital, and reach the train station. There, however, he was re-captured and brought back. His botched escape fueled the commissar's anger and one of his many political lessons to Umberto: "This is the extent of your capitalist intelligence: you believe even in what you do not see."[39] Eager to prove Soviet humanity toward the prisoners and the moral superiority of the Soviet order, in his recollections, Umberto emphasized that neither Ignat nor Dobrota was condemned to harsh punishments for their actions. What Umberto failed to mention is that thieving and attempting to escape could be acts of resistance against one's captors and ways to reclaim "a fragment of free identity."[40]

By demographic density, the Italian prisoners represented the third national group. A large room in ward no. 3 served as their headquarter, where they all slept except from doctors Landi and Filippi who were assigned to a small room next to it. While historians have described the conflicts that often emerged among Italian POWs in Soviet internment camps—and that could stem from reasons of either material or political nature—according to Umberto, the Italians were "the most carefree and cheerful" of all the hospital's inhabitants and those who more readily adapted to the condition of imprisonment.

---

[38]UM, commenti 26.8.1994. Anfisa, too, remembers that Ignat used to steal in the hospital. See UM, Anfisa to Umberto 18.8.1994.

[39]UM, commenti 16.10.1993, 30.10.1993, and 24.2.1994.

[40]Hynes, *The Soldiers' Tale*, 250. Liubov' Kharitonova remembers another attempted escape, by three prisoners who worked in the hospital's bakery. "Pochti vse nashi vrachi" http://www.zubova-poliana.narod.ru/warheros1-hospital4.htm.

They joked to normalize tragedy and, to fight homesickness, they organized improvised concerts using buckets and spoons as musical instruments, and singing popular melodies and love songs.[41] In his writings, Umberto fondly described some of his fellow Italian prisoners, such as the Abruzzian Lino Cellenza, nicknamed "the fat" because of his robust physique; a certain Bonvecchio from Trento, tall, thin, and always grumbling about something; the short and thin Vincenzo Diotaiuti, also from Abruzzo, who arrived at Zubova with a frostbitten gangrenous foot and was immediately subjected to the amputation of his right leg; and the two tailors from the South, Strizza and Peluso, who helped Anfisa in her duties as clothing warehouse manager. In many notes, Umberto also reminisced about the artilleryman Giovanni Tavan, from Forte dei Marmi (Lucca province). Orphaned since birth and unemployed, Tavan had joined Mussolini's Black Shirts at a young age and then volunteered to go to the Eastern front in the fascist assault unit "Tagliamento." When he arrived at Zubova, he was only eighteen, had a badly injured shoulder and frostbitten toes, which were immediately amputated by the Soviet surgeons. The hospital's personnel knew about his political standing, Umberto emphasized, but nonetheless cured him and eventually repatriated him.

The "Contradictions" of Soviet Life and Umberto's "Serious Illness"

The more Umberto knew, the more life in the camp appeared to him as filled with "contradictions." Some of them were nothing more than minor incongruencies, such as the political commissar's "phobia" that prisoners might concoct escape plans. Umberto had many times tried to convince him that escape was impossible for frail convalescent prisoners, especially given the barbed wire encircling the camp and the guards' strict surveillance. But the commissar Sergei, who was under

---

[41]UM, commenti 26.8.1994. On relationships among Italian prisoners in the Soviet camps see Giusti, *Stalin's Italian Prisoners*.

strict orders from above to prevent breakouts, never relinquished this fear. Yet—and this is what seemed paradoxical to Umberto—this very commissar often let groups of five or six prisoners take the linen to the laundry building outside the camp escorted by a single unarmed nurse. Similarly, he let some prisoners go to the near forest to cut wood or fetch water accompanied only by one armed guard. Allowed to go with them outside the fenced camp as the hospital's interpreter and even encouraged to do that by Polina (who insisted he should "breathe fresh air and stretch his legs"), Umberto knew that this situation could facilitate running away more than any plan possibly devised within his ward.[42] What he probably did not realize is that Sergei sanctioned the use of sick and disabled POWs beyond the hospital's fenced zone because he was *required* to utilize their labor.

Other "contradictions" were of a more profound nature, such as those surrounding the Soviet system and the Soviet people's character, especially their sense of obedience. Observing the hospital's daily life, Umberto noticed that "everything functioned" because any command given by a superior was duly followed without discussion. "Order and discipline" had been centerpieces of the fascist propaganda under which Umberto was brought up in Italy. Now he saw them ruling in the microcosm of communism that Zubova represented to him. He wrote, "[the hospital] was a well-functioning machine"; and the "Russians" "more precise, obedient, and conscientious than the Nazi soldiers." The "rigidity" of the Soviet system, Umberto argued in multiple notes, was its greatest strength and the biggest reason behind the Soviet victory over the Nazis.[43] Thus, despite Umberto's retrospective criticism of Fascism, ideas about order and discipline had cut deep in him. Like other ordinary Europeans of his generation, especially those who grew up in authoritarian regimes, he made a "nearly automatic association of normality and prosperity with order."[44] In addition,

---

[42]UM, commenti 2.7.1993.

[43]UM, commenti 5.7.1993 and 16.10.1993.

[44]Peter Fritzsche, *The Turbulent World of Franz Göll: An Ordinary Berliner Writes the Twentieth Century* (Cambridge: Harvard University Press, 2011), 201–2; and Biess, *Homecomings*, 113.

like some prisoners from other defeated countries, Umberto, too, was attracted to the Soviet system precisely because of the fall of Fascism and Italy's total capitulation.[45] Having disidentified with Mussolini's confidence in victory, he still effortlessly reproduced the fascist principle of authoritarian order in relation to the Soviet Union and with a clearly positive connotation.

Soviet "rigidity" meant that nobody had the luxury to be unemployed. Everybody was compelled to work, even more than eight hours a day, if the state considered it necessary. Besides labor, solidarity, too, was not a choice but a precept without exemption options. Umberto saw this with his own eyes one summer when a fire broke out in the neighboring collective farm "Red October," and everybody was mobilized to extinguish it. Not only the commanding sergeant and his guards but also the nurses and the prisoners were required to help. Furthermore, by order of the political commissar, a train coming from Riazan' was stopped and its passengers rallied to quench the "Red October" fire. Only when the fire was over were people sent back to their activities. Commenting on this episode, Umberto articulated admiration for the way in which roads and railways were blocked and passers-by ordered to help when the community was in danger. He wrote, "I think that systems such as this shouldn't be suppressed as traumatically [as it happened to the Soviet Union in 1991]."[46]

The Soviet people's lack of enthusiasm, however, made Umberto sometimes wonder whether blind obedience came from political "consciousness" or "fear of punishment." For instance, when prisoner Mariano Ruggeri stole a pillowcase and used its fabric to make small tobacco bags, Anfisa panicked that she might be punished because managing the scarce hospital's linen was her responsibility and those guilty of stealing socialist property were usually sentenced to serious punishments. Another example was the political commissar. He declared himself fortunate to participate in the construction of communism and, in Umberto's eyes, he seemed proud to inspire fear

---

[45]Muminov, *Eleven Winters.*
[46]UM, commenti, 13.2.1994 and 30.5.1994.

and intimidate everybody with his mere presence. Yet, he, too, at times appeared to act not out of belief but simply following orders coming from above. In Umberto's words, he was "a small omnipotent dictator in a small miserable village of evacuees whose only relative importance was to host sick POWs." What was the real extent of his agency and ability to take initiatives? Umberto had a hard time answering this question, but, ultimately, he decided it was irrelevant. "I cannot know whether [the Russian people] were satisfied or unsatisfied with communism. But, when I was interned, I saw order, discipline, and obedience. … Since I came back to my country …, I have not seen such a system anymore."[47]

Nonetheless, despite this retrospective appraisal for communist "order," Umberto's memoirs also betray that, while living in the hospital, he was deeply troubled by a "contradiction" that concerned his very survival. After the first months of 1943 (when a typhus epidemic had ravaged through the hospital and prisoners' death rate had reached twenty-five individuals a day), living conditions had steadily improved. Indeed, in May 1943, the NKVD issued order no. 248, detailing measures to be taken to reduce prisoners' mortality, bring all camps to better sanitary standards, and enhance the health care provided to each internee. According to what Umberto remembered, besides a ration of 600 grams of bread (white for those with gastric disorders and black for all the others), each prisoner at Zubova began also to be provided with sugar and generous amounts of a cheap tobacco (*makorka*). They also received cottage cheese (*tvorog*), millet porridge (*pshennaia kasha*), and butter. In addition, hospital officials allowed them to fish in the river Partsa and consume whatever they caught—a permission that helped compensate for missing food allocations at a time when Zubova might have been cut off from central food supplies.[48] Every seven to ten days, the captives

---

[47]UM, commenti, 5.7.1993 and 22.6.1994; AS, Umberto to Anfisa, 26.12.1998.

[48]AS, Umberto to Anfisa, 20.9.1993; email from Olga Avdiukova (Anfisa's granddaughter) dated 13.3.2023; and "Pochti vse nashi vrachi" http://www.zubova-poliana.narod.ru/warheros1-hospital4.htm. Order no. 248 decreed the distribution of "750 grams of bread per day, and a food ration increased by 25 percent until [prisoners'] ability to work was fully restored." Giusti, *Stalin's Italian Prisoners*, 81. See also, Alexopoulos, *Illness*, 40.

had access to a washroom, where they cleaned up using small pieces of soap—while feeling the female nurses' unembarrassed gazes on their bodies. Finally, far from being hated by the Soviet hospital workers or mistreated by the guards, the POWs increasingly enjoyed their compassion, which, Umberto insisted, every day manifested itself in silent acts of kindness. As he learned from prisoners coming from nearby camps and temporary held at Zubova for treatment, these conditions were much better than those ruling in the labor camps.

However, prisoners' lives seemed to be hanging on a thin thread as a "cult of mystery" informed life in the hospital and orders from above (*prikazy*) could unexpectedly upend their existences. His "friend" the commissar received these *prikazy* directly from Moscow and had power of life and death over anybody in the hospital. A word from him was enough to make anybody "disappear." In addition, a commission from the medical-sanitation department regularly came to Zubova to conduct special visits. The doctors making it up hurriedly determined the prisoners' physical fitness by checking the state of their buttocks' muscles, and, if they found them fit for work, immediately shipped them to a labor camp.[49] Lastly, while the deaths had certainly decreased, anybody who died was still unceremoniously undressed (to remove any sign of identification) and stacked "like dead branches" under the convalescence ward's outdoor staircase, where the cold helped to preserve the corpses before they would be buried in the common pit outside the camp.[50] In his position as the camp's interpreter, Umberto witnessed Zubova's constant juxtaposition of "normal" and "abnormal," and greatly struggled to understand it. Were his Soviet captors the cynical perpetrators of barbarities? Or were they just moved by the harsh exigencies of the time? Uncapable to find clear-cut answers to these questions, he ended up developing traumatic responses to them.

The episode of his "sudden and serious illness" in the Spring of 1945 is particularly illuminating. Through his narration of this episode, we see that Umberto did not understand prisoners' health

---

[49]This procedure is confirmed by other Gulag memoirists, too. See Alexopoulos, *Illness*, 65.
[50]UM, commenti 30.1.1994, 22.6.1994, and 26.8.1994.

comprehensively, that is to include both physical and psychological well-being. When he claimed that "the Russians" had cured him, he mostly thought about his body. At the same time, Umberto's writings also indicate that he was keenly aware of the psychological nature of his suffering and, at times, ready to make sense of it through psychoanalytical frames—which he had never formally apprehended but which he seemed to intuitively grasp.

Umberto's ailment manifested itself in the inability to move, a widespread fragility, a dull pain in the stomach, and the refusal to eat any food. The hospital's doctors excluded a tuberculosis relapse, but they could not diagnose what exactly afflicted him and just kept him under close medical observation. Polina visited him every time she could and the nurse on shift checked on him even two or three times a night. Once, seeing Umberto deeply despondent and heartsick, Polina tried to convince him to eat by promising she would bring him anything he desired. But, when asked what he wanted, Umberto briskly replied "a bit of sun from Italy." Increasingly worried about his beloved—and perhaps suspecting that his disease was a malady of the soul—Polina at a certain point arranged to place Umberto in a small room with only one other prisoner of his choice as roommate and helper. To perform this role, Umberto picked a certain Redolescu, the only Romanian prisoner he was fond of because of his sensitivity and the only one he trusted because of his personal loyalty to him. Redolescu's "attentiveness, diligence, and above all patience" created an empathic environment for Umberto, thereby helping him begin to repair the traumas he was experiencing and, in the end, recover from the most serious physical manifestations of them.[51]

If we look at Umberto's "serious sickness" from the perspective of trauma studies, we immediately see that he had become ill due to emotional stress. Psychological research on former POWs has stressed the corrosive effects of long-term confinement, popularly called

---

[51]UM, commenti 16.10.1993. Nowhere in his writings does Umberto explain why he did not select a fellow Italian as roommate.

"barbed-wire disease," arising from years of isolation.[52] Similarly, studies of soldiers' emotions have shown that men detailed to foreign lands frequently felt profound melancholy, while recent work on Gulag medicine has revealed that "prisoners struggled to keep their mental balance" in the camps.[53] Whereas Umberto was lucky enough to find affection and, perhaps, sexual solace in Polina's arms, for him like for other twentieth-century soldiers, feelings of moroseness, unwillingness to recover, and self-destructive behaviors derived from a combination of negative factors, all of which wreaked emotional havoc on his psyche. He did not know how events were unfolding on the front lines or back in Italy and lacked any information on when he would be released; he longed for a warmer climate while all around him was only cold and snow; and he could not rationalize his feelings toward the Soviet people due to the incongruities he constantly observed. As he put it, in the back of his mind was fascist propaganda, but in front of his eyes "the enemy" was curing his body and making all possible efforts to save his life.[54] It might well have been that he developed some degree of emotional dependence on Polina and, like internees in other contexts, felt drawn to his captor the commissar Sergei.

The soldiers' self-imposed veto on talking about the war further contributed to Umberto's depression. At Zubova, the prisoners used to talk about their families and homes, their regional traditions, and their local recipes; often, they compared notes on how they baked the bread or cooked different types of meat. But they never talked about the battles in which they had fought, the places where each of them had been captured, or how they had been injured. Umberto did not even know if any of the POWs in his ward had walked in the snow together with him or had been crammed in his same prisoners'

---

[52]Joël Kotek and Pierre Rigoulot, *Das Jahrhundert der Lager: Gefangenschaft, Zwangsarbeit, Vernichtung* (Berlin: Propyläen, 2001); and Herman, *Trauma*.

[53]Hanna, *Your Death Would Be Mine*; Scheck *Love between Enemies*; and Healey, *Gulag Doctors*, 210. See also Ben Shephard's chapter "Prisoner of War," in *A War of Nerves: Soldiers and Psychiatrists in the Twentieth Century* (Cambridge, MA: Harvard University Press, 2001), 313–24.

[54]UM, commenti 16.10.1993.

convoy train. This self-imposed silence was not uncommon among camps' internees. Its most nefarious consequence was that it prevented POWs from engaging in any healing narrative that externalized their psychological traumas. The Zubova prisoners, in other words, were survivors incapable of communicating their experience; this incapacity compounded the negative repercussions of battlefield trauma. It was not a coincidence that Umberto began to heal when he was able to confide in Redolescu.

Fifty years later, when Umberto reminisced about this episode in his correspondence with Anfisa, he regretted his behavior in the hospital and put the blame for his "sickness" on himself. How could he be annoyed by Polina's visits? How could he "sadistically vex" his "doctor-angel" by refusing to eat and asking her to bring him "a bit of sun from Italy"? In hindsight, Umberto assessed the care he received at Zubova as better than any medical treatment he could possibly receive in an Italian hospital, even in a first-class one. His "moral suffering" of the time now seemed "unjustified" and "for nothing," as proven by the fact that he did return to Italy. This was a retrospective interpretation motivated by his overwhelming desire to undo Italian prejudices against the Soviet Union.[55] Driven by this motivation, Umberto was unable to present any critical perspective on imprisonment's outcome for his mental health, namely that imprisonment itself generated traumas. When he insisted that the "Russians" cured him, missing from his definition of health are any considerations about the mental breakdowns resulting from the prolonged suffering and deprivation of captivity. Even though he made references to the "depressive crisis" that continued after his repatriation, he wanted to connect his mental disturbances narrowly to the corporeal and psychological horrors of the front. At the same time, however, when Umberto pointed the finger for his suffering at the indefiniteness and indeterminacy of internment life, he unwittingly aligned his interpretation with Freud's view of anxiety. And when he wrote that, in the end, there was nothing to fear for POWs, he echoed Kierkegaard's and Heidegger's definition

---

[55]UM, commenti, 16.10.1993.

of anxious feelings as "the fear of something that is nothing."[56] As we know from that literature, only when the individual can locate something specific to fear is he/she able to allay anxiety. Umberto's insistence that his "moral suffering" ultimately was "for nothing" and that his fears were "unjustified" betrayed not only his commitment to a positive representation of the Soviet Union but also his struggle to work through trauma.

* * *

Umberto enjoyed an exceptional position at the Zubova Poliana prisoner hospital. He moved quite freely inside and outside of it; he entertained a romantic liaison (whether sexual or only platonic) with one of the hospital's doctors; and his job as interpreter made him valuable to many people. All this protected him from abuses. It also facilitated his access to knowledge amidst the general atmosphere of secrecy and other prisoners' doubts about the information they were fed. His interactions with the hospital's diverse inhabitants (and most importantly his special relationship with his "friend" the commissar Sergei) gave him more opportunities than others had to attempt to comprehend the world in which he lived. And yet, that world's "contradictions" bothered him deeply and ultimately reduced him to a state of "dark pessimism" and death wish.

Umberto's memories of Zubova Poliana offer an invaluable intimate glimpse of daily life in a Soviet prisoners' hospital. Certainly, his experience was both singular at that time and colored by how he wanted to remember and tell it in hindsight. Yet, his testimony about it preserves a sharp capacity to illuminate the "normality" of internment and the circumstances that might have facilitated or hindered this "normality." With all the caveats of political indoctrination, authorial intent, and nostalgia, Umberto's story powerfully tests the nature of suffering in Soviet internment and the extent to which captivity was only about that.

---

[56]LaCapra, *Writing History,* 57.

CHAPTER 5
THE UNHEALING WOUNDS OF WAR

In early Summer 1945, a Soviet State Defense Committee's directive signed directly by Stalin authorized the NKVD to "release from the camps and special hospitals and to repatriate prisoners of war who cannot be used as labor because of their physical condition: invalids, the chronically ill, the debilitated and the long-term disabled, 225,000 men in all."[1] Later, on August 10, Beria sent Stalin a plan involving the release of an additional 708,000 soldiers and non-commissioned officers. Following these resolutions, mass prisoner repatriations started in September 1945 and slowly progressed until the mid-1950s. For Italy, they ultimately led to the return of 21,065 POWs: 10,035 were ARMIR's veterans, while 11,033 were soldiers interned by the Germans after Italy switched sides in September 1943 and later transferred to areas controlled by the Soviet Union.[2]

Returning home with one of the first repatriation waves, Umberto had a hard time reintegrating into Italian society and faced multiple challenges in demanding pensions, adequate physical and mental healthcare, and an opportunity for his distinct experience to be incorporated into public discourse. He could not fit back into peacetime life not only because of the country's general poverty, devastation, and demoralization but also because he could not express his memories. Although he eventually regained a measure of social stability after the disruptions of the war years, he remained forever scarred by the traumas inflicted on him by military conflict and internment. Concluding Umberto's story with an overview of his return to Italy and post-repatriation life, this chapter invites reflection

---

[1] As quoted in Giusti, *Stalin's Italian Prisoners*, 185.
[2] Ibid., 186–200.

on soldiers' complicated returns to normalcy and what the frontiers of memory and citizenship were for them in the context of postwar Italy.

Repatriation

To Zubova Poliana, the repatriation order arrived unexpectedly and was executed hastily. With Umberto by his side doing the necessary translations, the political commissar announced that prisoners of all nationalities, except the Germans and others who had fought in the Wehrmacht, would be repatriated and should prepare to leave immediately. Of course, the announcement created a lot of confusion as, despite the commissar's repeated calls to keep calm, the prisoners could not repress their euphoria. Many cried; some thanked God; others hugged those who stood next to them; and a few began to sing. The commissar tried to hush them but did not seem too irritated. The only patently annoyed person that day was Nastia Golikova, a nurse well known in the camp for her hatred toward all the prisoners. Her vicious *bon voyage* sounded like a curse and Umberto still clearly remembered it fifty years later: "there are some rivers in Russia that your convoy must cross. I wish that one of their bridges will collapse."[3]

The order from Moscow stated that all prisoners who could walk were allowed to repatriate. Leaning on rudimentary crutches, the camp's amputees claimed their right to join the departing column, while a blind internee asked a comrade to guide him. The commissar wanted as many prisoners as possible to go. Only the officers should not be repatriated, and they would indeed stay interned until July 1946. When this news was announced, Umberto saw Landi and Filippi's joy turn first into incredulity and then desperate sadness.

Standing at the entrance of ward no. 3, commissar Sergei called out the prisoners' names in a metallic voice. When they passed by him, he personally frisked each of them and dispossessed them of any object that might carry information about Zubova. When Umberto's turn came, Sergei attempted to keep him in the Soviet Union. First,

---

[3]UM, commenti 30.5.1994.

he insinuated that polyglot Umberto might be an officer working for the fascist secret police (*Opera Vigilanza Repressione Antifascismo*, or OVRA). Then, switching the stick for the carrot, he renewed his proposal that Umberto go to Moscow, renounce Italian citizenship, and acquire a Soviet one. This time, Umberto responded that he agreed but first wanted to go to Italy and check on his parents. The commissar did not like his answer. He searched Umberto, too, just like the other POWs, and, having stripped him of his belongings, ordered him to join the others walking to the train station.

But Umberto was no ordinary POW, not even in the circumstances of repatriation. On the train taking him and his fellow prisoners to the end of the Russian railway line at Râmnicu Sărat, in Eastern Romania, he had second thoughts about Sergei's proposal and the way he had answered to it. Umberto wanted to stay in Russia and was considering jumping off the train wagon. It was Polina who prevented him from doing that. Indeed, according to the repatriation order, besides the escorting officers, Soviet health personnel were also supposed to accompany the prisoners' convoy to guarantee for their health until they found themselves on Soviet territory.[4] Polina had volunteered to play that role. When Umberto told her about his intention to escape, she dissuaded him and made sure he went all the way to the transition camp of Râmnicu Sărat where the Italian POWs descended the train and underwent quarantine for two weeks. At that point, Polina's assignment as the accompanying doctor was completed and she had to go back to Zubova to flank Landi and Filippi in taking care of the German prisoners still kept in the hospital. Umberto saw her one last time two or three days into the quarantine, when she called him to her office to give him some medicine for the rest of the trip. As he confessed to Anfisa later, "I instinctually wanted to hug and kiss her! But there was a Russian soldier who might have seen us, so I only kissed her hand ... I was sure I would have seen her again."[5] As we know, this would not be the case. Umberto and Polina separated forever on that day at Râmnicu Sărat.

---

[4] Giusti, *Stalin's Italian Prisoners*, 188.
[5] AS, Umberto to Anfisa 14.3.1994.

Soviet Internment

After the two-week quarantine, the POWs embarked on another train, this time running on European tracks (i.e., with a different, shorter track gauge) and taking them to Prague. Finally, a third train transported them to Frankfurt and, after yet another quarantine, a last convoy took them to Italy, to a recovery hospital in Merano. In Frankfurt, however, Umberto and two other Italian POWs were recruited to help the Soviet officers sell food supplies on the German black market where the supplies could be profitably exchanged for jewels, clothes, and pieces of furniture. For the starving Germans, Umberto commented, "bread was like gold," and the Red Army officers did not want to miss the opportunity to speculate on that. The other two prisoners were used to carry the goods, while Umberto—who was too weak to lift any weight—served as their interpreter. In this role, he spent one week in Frankfurt and then followed the Soviet officers to Berlin where, Umberto explained, they all enjoyed more bartering dealings and other unsavory "adventures."

> How did I spend one month in Germany with the Russian sergeant and the Russian officer? Well!!! Since I was young … I looked for adventures. The Russian sergeant and officer helped me and all together we found adventures. … In the evenings, they stayed back in the hotel but gave me a full pocket of money and I went to buy vodka and girls. … My friend the sergeant got a little venereal disease. It was dangerous for him to go to the Russian military doctor. And so, I accompanied him to the French zone. The French doctor gave him medication.[6]

After a month of this life, when all the food had been exchanged for valuables, Umberto's captors (or accomplices?) traveled back to the Soviet Union and left him free to go back home.

---

[6] AS, commenti al foglio matricolare.

Figure 5.1 Umberto when he came back from internment.

"Moral Bewilderment" and the Struggle for Reintegration

The first years after repatriation were a time of disquiet, recklessness, and anger for Umberto: he could neither resume his fascist pre-war routines nor simply slip back into peacetime life. How unfamiliar Bolzano and its inhabitants must have appeared to him after those three years in the Soviet Union! Looking back at his repatriation, he commented that he had brought home "a body that carried the inexorable signs of disease and hardship" and "a spirit that was sapped, filled with delusion, regret, and … a lot of memories." In his mid-twenties, Umberto was limping and could not walk for more than 100–200 meters. He also suffered from acute back pain and "chronic bronchitis." More crucially, he felt that his mind was in a state of "confusion" and "moral bewilderment." He could not find motivation in anything, stopped trusting his fellow human beings, and even convinced himself that "peace brings monotony." An "unquenchable revenge spirit" drove him as he blamed the war for having taken the best years of his youth. Yet, he also felt apathetic and afraid to experience new disappointments.[7]

It was not uncommon for returning soldiers to feel thoroughly alienated from their old ways of living. On the one hand, they were exhausted by the sufferings and exertions of the war years. On the other hand, in all its gruesomeness, the war's violence and endless succession of hardships had somehow given their lives meaning and direction. Especially for those who had experienced the trauma of a long captivity, active engagement with the postwar world was particularly difficult. Subsiding into their new peaceful existences, just like Umberto, many other demobilized soldiers and former POWs were nostalgic for war's energy and high excitement, while also feeling passive toward their present.[8]

On top of that, over the years of Umberto's imprisonment, much had changed in Italy. "The country," one scholar writes, "became a republic, a new democratic constitution was introduced, women were enfranchised, and national elections were held that led to the durable ascendancy of two parties—the Christian Democrats and the Communists—that were emphatically different from the major political forces of the past."[9] But Umberto had not witnessed any of this. He had neither participated in the Resistance nor felt the cheerfulness that followed liberation. The collapse of the fascist structures of government and the election of Italy's new government had happened without his input and the chronology of his return to normality was different from that of his fellow citizens. Quite obviously, this situation resulted in psychological and social displacement for him and many other repatriates (and not only in the Italian context).[10] Umberto grew ever resentful that his countrymen neither appreciated the sacrifices

---

[7]UM, "Sorvolando," "Reminescenze," and commenti 30.5.1994; AS, Umberto to Anfisa 26.11.1993.

[8]LaCapra, *Writing History*; Herman, *Trauma*; and Hynes, *The Soldiers' Tale*.

[9]Martin Conway, *Western Europe Democratic Age:1945–1968* (Princeton: Princeton University Press, 2020), 36.

[10]Carlo Ferroni, *Italian POWs Speak Out at Last* (Amherst: Teneo, 2013); Goltermann, *War in Their Minds*; Muminov, *Eleven Winters*; and Biess, *Homecomings*.

veterans had made nor were able to acknowledge and address the magnitude of the war's psychological impact on them.

Despite these feelings, a few years after his return, Umberto dutifully fell into the familial and professional responsibilities that postwar Italy demanded from him as a male citizen. In 1949, he married his girlfriend Licia and had two children with her. His knowledge of foreign languages helped him land a job in the Bolzano post office, which he held until 1956. Later, he frequently changed jobs but was nonetheless always able to bring home a living a wage and support his family as the only breadwinner. On the surface, Italian society had successfully reclaimed him as a functioning man. Yet, fatherhood, gainful employment, and all the other trappings of middle-class domesticity and decency were not enough for Umberto to "put order" in his life.[11] The former POW never fully emerged from the abyss of war and internment. He also never completely reconciled with the course of Italian history.

Umberto's desperate search for Polina sharply dramatizes the sense of inadequacy that he continued to feel throughout his post-Russia life, revealing that his supposedly regained masculinity and normality were in fact shot through with the traumas he had experienced. Missing his beloved doctor and hoping to reconnect with her, immediately after his return Umberto began to send letters to the address she had given him when they separated in Romania: "camp post office no. 19." We do not know if any of these letters reached Polina and if she ever attempted to reply to them. What is certain, however, is that Umberto received neither responses nor his own letters back. Over the years, he came to believe that the tension caused by the Cold War made it impossible for him to reestablish personal relations with anybody in the Soviet Union. Yet, he did not give up. In 1961, when "the political situation seemed more favorable," Umberto wrote to the Italian and Soviet Red Cross agencies, the Italian embassy in Moscow, and the Soviet one in Rome. Sadly, none of these offices gave him the information he was looking for. Then, in 1981, when the world chess championship took place in Merano, just thirty kilometers north of Bolzano, Umberto

---

[11]UM, commenti, 30.10.1993.

went there in the hope to speak with the Soviet players. Of course, he could not possibly approach them, but he did manage to speak with a journalist of the press agency *Novosti* [News], a certain Alexei Hazov, who was at that time based in Rome. Hazov seemed interested in helping Umberto and asked all possible questions about Polina. A few years later, however, he informed Umberto that his searches, too, had failed.[12] "Not even a needle," complained a disheartened and increasingly angry Umberto, "could go through that Curtain." Crucially, even after he found out that Polina had passed away, he still could not give her a proper (metaphorical) burial. "Pavlina should have never died," he wrote in multiple letters to Anfisa.[13] In Freudian terms, one might say that depressed and traumatized Umberto was locked in the compulsive act of searching for Polina, while Polina herself had become a ghost, a haunting presence resisting disappearance. Unable to mourn her, Umberto could not fully engage his traumas.

Also revealing of Umberto's difficult struggle to reintegrate (and hardly unique to him as a veteran) was his quest to gain full rights as war invalid. Umberto had officially been identified as "missing in action" since December 14, 1942. Based on this designation, in August 1943, his father Augusto had applied for the so-called *Presenza alle Bandiere*, an economic arrangement whereby the families of soldiers missing in action received a pension for a limited period of twelve months. It was a means to compensate for the severe blow to Italian families' sustenance caused by the prolonged absence of their males for war service. And, indeed, it was on this pension of 300 liras a month that the Montinis survived between May 1944 (when the *podesta'* of Bolzano began paying it) and April 1945. When Umberto came home in October 1945, not only had the pension's money long finished but, adding insult to injury, his parents were asked to return the received pension back to the state because their son in the end

---

[12]Museo Storico Italiano della Guerra, uncatalogued Fondo Umberto Montini, letter exchange between Montini and Hazov.
[13]AS, Umberto to Anfisa 16-28.1.1994 and 20.9.1993; and UM, commenti 14.5.1994.

Figure 5.2 Polina in 1977–8.

turned out to be still alive.[14] The families of many other Italian POWs went through something similar because the Italian state prioritized Resistance fighters in drafting war pension schemes and, until 1950, did not finalize its welfare and compensation legislation for former prisoners.[15] Umberto's writings on this absurd situation betray all the anger and frustration he felt immediately upon his return home.

Even more upsetting, however, was his first official encounter with the postwar Italian state at the Bolzano military district. Military bureaucracy required each returnee to undergo *discriminazione*. Deriving from the Latin *discrimire* (to tell the difference), this term

---

[14]Archivio Storico del Comune di Bolzano, Fondo Leva e Affari Militari, serie Presenti alle Bandiere. Augusto Montini's petition to the Podesta' of Bolzano dated 10.8.1943 and the Podesta' response dated 31.5.1944.

[15]Maria Teresa Brancaccio, "Where Have All the Traumatized People Gone? World War II and Its Aftermath in Italy: Trauma and Oblivion," in *The Politics of War Trauma: The Aftermath of World War Two in Eleven European Countries*, ed. Jolande Withuis and Annet Mooij (Amsterdam: Aksant, 2010), 141–65.

indicated a clearance process that distinguished the good, loyal, politically uncompromised, and anti-communist POWs from those who might have collaborated with the enemy and developed pro-communist sympathies. In line with it, Umberto was interviewed by a higher-ranking officer and asked to fill out some forms. When he was asked, "How have you been treated during imprisonment?," Umberto gingerly answered, "Well. The Russians cured us, gave us food, and loved us." Without hesitation, the interviewing officer accused Umberto of being a communist and stated that he would not clear him unless Umberto changed his declaration concerning the treatment he had received at Zubova. The denial of military clearance would in turn lead to a denial of veteran and disability benefits, but Umberto was unwilling to "spit in the face of a people who had cured [him] and repatriated [him]," and thus preferred to give up on the clearance. This, as he recounted later in his memoirs, was the first instance in which his voice was silenced and the beginning of his struggle for both "the truth" and his social rights.[16]

Discriminazione shows that political vetting was a criterion for welfare entitlement because the Italian postwar state secured or discounted claims based on how repatriated POWs remembered their internment. In postwar Japan, too, the so-called Red repatriates were not only excluded from the victim discourse of their country's history but also forced to engage in long fights to receive some compensation for their lost years.[17] In both countries, former POWs' positive memory of the Soviet Union was perceived as loyalty to that country and as such compromised the veterans in the eyes of their compatriots. Not only Italian and Japanese but also West German societies just wanted to move on and leave behind—or selectively remember—the nightmare of Fascism/Imperialism/Nazism. In addition, their public cultures were percolated by fears of communism and a strong animosity between their communist and pro-capitalist parties. Returnees' experiences and memories of Soviet captivity

---

[16]UM, commenti, 16.10.1993; and AS, Umberto to Anfisa, 10.2.1994.
[17]Muminov, *Eleven Winters.*

were especially significant in a divided Germany, when both the GDR and FRG "defined their postwar identities largely with respect to the Soviet Union."[18] In Italy, the bitter struggle between the Italian Communist Party (PCI) and the Christian Democracy Party (DC) ripped the electorate apart. Those ex-prisoners who denounced the poor conditions of Soviet custody became the source of a political campaign in which former *fuoriusciti*—now members of the PCI— were accused of not having done enough to save their fellow citizens. But the voices of those who reminded Italians that their country had been an aggressor in the Second World War were uneasy to accommodate.[19]

Umberto was trapped right in the middle of these memory wars. Immediately after his repatriation, he had attempted to share his positive memory of Zubova not only with the officers of the Bolzano military district but also with some neighbors. However, when they responded by accusing him of being "a liar, an insane person, and a communist," he had stopped talking to them. He also decided not to stay in touch with other former prisoners and became unwilling to talk publicly about his war and internment experiences. Feeling that his memory did not fit with the official narrative crafted by the Italian state, he chose silence, solitude, and withdrawal. In truth, he did reconstruct his wartime story for his parents and brothers, and then for his wife Licia and his children Aldo and Erminia, but the imposed, strictly private character of his acts of remembrance and narration made him feel resentful and unappreciated, as though all the suffering he had lived through was worth nothing. He wrote, "we [former POWs] were not forgiven our survival. We were looked upon as rare beasts who had escaped a cataclysm. We were tolerated but asked to be quiet and forget the past."[20]

---

[18]Biess, *Homecomings*, 6.

[19]Dzhordzho Skotoni, "Kampaniia protiv ital'ianskikh 'antipatrioticheskikh ofitserov': sud nad veteranom russkogo fronta kapitanom Lamberti iz-za vystupleniia v zashchitu SSSR," *Istoriia. Vestnik Nizhnegorodskogo universiteta* 2 (2016): 95–100; and Antonelli, "La Campagna di Russia."

[20]AS, Umberto to Anfisa 29.5.1996; and UM, commenti, 30.1.1994.

As an intensely political form of welfare that identified and excluded communist sympathizers, *discriminazione* also worked as a gatekeeping device with specific symbolic and material consequences for POWs with disabilities. Only in 1960, after multiple visits by military doctors in the neighboring cities of Trento and Verona, was Umberto recognized as "war invalid of the third category," a designation that entitled him to a pension and guaranteed him permanent employment. The former POW considered the money that he received from the Italian state to be a "compensation of the damage" caused to him by the war. This "compensation," he argued, was his right because he had not gone to war as a volunteer and because he had lost his health in the war: he was an innocent victim of Fascism who had gained nothing but suffering from it. On the one hand, Umberto was proud of his small military pension. He felt that he had "earned" it "through [his] suffering and pain," and would not allow his wife to "touch" it (although she administered all other sources of income in their household, including his employment pension). On the other hand, however, with the third category of invalidity Umberto could access for free only the general medical services offered in state hospitals, while still having to pay for the specialized therapies he needed to recover his mobility and improve his breathing. Had Umberto tried to access mental health therapy, the miserly amount of this pension would have not been enough.

Even more crucially, the few liras that he received as war invalid of the third category made him feel "guilty to be alive."[21] Because monetary compensation is a recognition of a person's suffering, which anchors this suffering in public memory, Umberto rightfully saw this small pension as a symbolic denial of his bodily and psychic wounds: it was as if Italy was trying to erase his disability from the country's collective memory.[22] The feeling of injustice never abandoned him and, throughout his life, Umberto kept submitting requests for a more just pensioning arrangement. When in February 1992 the Italian Treasury

---

[21] AS, Umberto to Anfisa 20.3.1995; and UM, commenti, 30.10.1993.
[22] Dan Diner and Gotthart Wunberg, eds., *Restitution and Memory: Material Restauration in Europe* (New York and Oxford: Berghahn Books, 2007).

Ministry raised Umberto's pension to the second category on grounds of his poor health, he thought this was a mockery and immediately filed another complaint to be assigned the first category. After another series of medical examinations and multiple rejections, his request was finally approved in January 1998. While the Soviet Union had classified him as invalid as soon as he had arrived at Zubova, it took over fifty years to the Italian state to acknowledge that his tuberculosis and "grave pulmonary insufficiency" were strong enough reasons to grant him the highest rank of disability (so-called *superinvalidita'*). The official paperwork did not even mention his impaired mobility or his damaged mental health.[23]

Looking back at all of this, Umberto remembered the "prescient" words with which commissar Sergei had once warned him: "You deluded yourself with Fascism. Perhaps, you will delude yourself also with that freedom that you seek and will not find." Poorly received after his return, not materially helped to reintegrate into Italian society, and offered no psychological assistance in adapting to postwar life, Umberto joined the ranks of those survivors who, the Italian veteran and essayist Nuto Revelli wrote, "have a deep, hidden mark; are sick, tired, old; are falling apart. They all had the right to a pension, but pensioning bureaucracy is a wall you cannot pass."[24] As the fissure between him and the Italian state grew wider, Umberto not only began to see himself as a double victim (of the fascist government and of the current one) but also more broadly realized that the commissar was "not completely wrong" when he challenged the legitimacy of Western democracy. For the elderly veteran, democracy came to mean only instability, never-ending cycles of political elections, governmental coalitions that lasted merely one year, and "a useless waste of money" for which "the people" had to pay. We should bear in mind that both in the first years after Umberto's repatriation and when he wrote his memoirs, the political situation in Italy was considerably

---

[23]UM, determinazione no. 3602702 of the Italian Treasure Ministry dated May 28, 1998; and Umberto Montini, "Per favore non speculiamo sulle vittime dell'Armir," *Alto Adige*, 29.3.1992.
[24]Revelli, *La strada*, xii.

unstable: general elections were held four times between 1946 and 1948, and three times between 1992 and 1996. "Too much freedom and lack of discipline," Umberto averred, were the fertile ground on which mafia organizations thrived, the rich practiced tax fraud with impunity, class divisions increased, and materialism and individualism triumphed. If this was freedom and democracy, Umberto would gladly give it up to go back to Zubova.[25]

Working through Trauma

Jacques Lacan and others drawing on his work have recognized writing as a means of recreating one's shattered Self after violence and thereby undertake a healing process.[26] While Umberto's physical wounds were diagnosed, treated, and partially compensated, his psychic ones never received a formal diagnosis and, consequently, remained without treatment and compensation. As we have seen throughout this book, Umberto variously self-diagnosed, identifying multiple layers and forms of trauma in his psyche and recognizing their shifting nature. I would also suggest that in the last decade of his life, he attempted to self-treat by externalizing trauma and converting it into language.

Umberto's recollections, letters to Anfisa, and comments to Anfisa's letters were all forms of healing narrative directed at an audience. In the letters, he talked to Anfisa (the "magnificent woman" and the "saint" to whom he could freely "reveal his soul"). In the *commenti*, he talked to a potential editor who, Umberto hoped, would become complicit in the writing process by integrating all his notes into a seamless narrative (and thereby serving as analyst?). And in the memoirs, he talked to the larger audience of Italians (who in Umberto's imagination would eagerly read his story once it was polished and published). His nonlinear, sensory-oriented, and phantasmagoric

---

[25]UM, commenti 2.7.1993; AS, Umberto to Anfisa, 28.2.1996 and undated letter probably from the summer 1996.

[26]Jacques Lacan, *The Language of the Self: The Function of Language in Psychoanalysis*. Trans. Anthony Wilden (Baltimore: Johns Hopkins Press, 1968).

narration was both acutely painful—traumatizing in itself—and therapeutic to his wounded Self.[27] While he felt "apathetic, torpid, depressed, and disgusted by the world around him," the act of writing became the only means to give meaning to his otherwise "useless calvary." He wrote, "wounds that never healed reopen, yet the timid tears that well up in my eyes ... are necessary: they are beneficial and healthy."[28]

Umberto's "working through" trauma, however, had some "limits."[29] This is clearly revealed by the language he used in his Russian correspondence with Anfisa. He wrote that he was "homesick for Russia," "love[d] Russia," and desperately wanted to be again in the old, "better Russia" of the pre-perestroika period. "So many times," he announced in March 1994, "my thoughts flow to Zubova Poliana and my lips kiss [Polina's] picture." "Constantly," Umberto declared to Anfisa, "when I eat pasta ... and when I drink coffee, I think about Russia." "My head is in Russia, and there, in the background, I see our unforgettable Polina! ... Why did I come back to Italy?" Conversing with Anfisa and using their relationship as a means to relive his life at Zubova, Umberto collapsed the distinction between then and now, between a past to be represented in memory and a present to be invested in. Like other survivors, he felt the "permanent duality" of those who lead "parallel existence[s]," but, for him, the most compelling reality was that of Zubova.[30] His experience of the present was somehow blurred, while his intense memories of the past always intruded in his daily life.[31] Excluded by Italian society, Umberto also chose self-isolation by hiding in a room that he called "my Russian museum." (Indeed, he had turned the site of writing in his apartment into a memorial space, a place where he simultaneously relieved himself of his memory burden and relished the impossibility to

---

[27]Dori Laub, "Bearing Witness or the Vicissitudes of Listening," in *Testimony: Crises of Witnessing in Literature, Psychoanalysis, and History*, ed. Shoshanna Feldman and Dori Laub, (New York: Routledge, Chapman and Hall, 1992), 57–74.
[28]UM, commenti 14.5.1994, 30.5.1994, 8.3.1994, 13.2.1994; and "Reminescenze."
[29]On the "limits of working through" trauma see LaCapra, *Writing History*.
[30]Langer, *Holocaust Testimonies*, 95.
[31]Herman, *Trauma*, 90.

Figure 5.3 Umberto in his "Russian museum."

forget.) He did not know how to answer his wife's accusations that he loved Russia more than his own family and, when indiscrete neighbors battered him for not having grandchildren, he responded that he had a granddaughter in Saint Petersburg (i.e., Polina's granddaughter Aniuta). Writing in 1994, he often dated his letters "1944." In addition, he felt to be Russian because "first Polina and then all of you [Russians] helped me be born again." While other returnees used the concept of rebirth to describe the moment of homecoming, Umberto desired to have a different identity than the Italian one he was born into and imagined to be in a different world, far away from an Italy that, in his opinion, was not the democratic and free country that it purported to be. This Russian identity in turn set the story he wrote apart from other accounts of the same period: only he knew the "truth."[32]

* * *

---

[32]AS, Umberto to Anfisa 9.4.1993, 20.9.1993, 10.2.1994, 29.5.1995, 21.1.1997; and UM, commenti 13.2.1994, 11.4.1994 and 24.2.1994.

Reading Umberto's autobiographical installments, letters, and notes, we clearly see that neither the wounds inflected by the acute trauma of war nor those deriving from the prolonged trauma of captivity had ever fully healed for him. And yet equally clear is the force with which Umberto made his dissonant voice heard and accomplished many of his goals. He constructed a counter-memory of the Second World War and the Soviet Union that negotiated and often defied Italian official narratives, and that urged his readers to see how their past (Fascism and the Cold War) defined their very identity in the present. He also situated himself in both Italian and Russian history in ways that made his personal past usable. By juxtaposing descriptive accounts of events with portraits that elucidated and justified his course of life, he described the transformation that war and captivity had effected on him and thus developed an acceptable *Bildungsroman* schema: from young—and allegedly clueless—fascist to mature man mistrusting all political parties. Furthermore, his act of naming the dead to the living, which marked all his three sets of writings, both enabled relatives to learn the fate of their loved ones and helped him tackle his guilt for having survived.[33]

Umberto's intricate relationship between memory and trauma ultimately provides us with the opportunity to explore the mechanisms through which individuals navigate the aftermath of experiences such as war atrocities and internment. It also allows to recognize that both memory and trauma are not static entities but rather dynamic constructs evolving over time as individuals employ various coping strategies and memorializing practices. Finally, through the immediate resonance of Umberto's autobiographical writings, we appreciate the ways in which individual reckoning with a traumatic past is subject to a complex interplay of socio-political and cultural factors. Because of all of that, through Umberto's story, we are pushed to rethink our own historical memory of key twentieth-century events and ask questions about our present. Especially for those of us trying

---

[33]See also James Young, *The Texture of Memory. Holocaust Memorials and Meaning* (New Haven, CT: Yale University Press, 1993).

to understand the complexities of Russian society, where the legacies of authoritarianism and armed conflicts still persist, this book has hopefully offered a framework to reflect on the political trajectories of ordinary Europeans and why some of them came to identify all politics as "dirty," became skeptical of democracy, and developed nostalgia for dictators supposedly able to deal with conflicting group interests.

GLOSSARY OF FOREIGN TERMS

Alto Adige South Tyrol

Altoatesino (plural altoatesini) South Tyrolean

Armata Italiana in Russia, or ARMIR Italian Army in Russia

Avanguardista (plural avanguardisti) Italian men between fourteen and eighteen years old belonging to the ranks of the fascist youth organizations

Caporale corporal

Corpo di Spedizione Italiano in Russia, or CSIR Italian Expeditionary Corps in Russia

Davai come on, forward. "*davai* march" is the term used in Italian memoir literature to indicate the transfers of prisoners from the sites of capture at the front to the various labor camps and POWs hospitals in the interior

Democrazia Cristiana, DC Christian Democracy Party

Discriminazione military clearance process that distinguished between loyal POWs and those who might have collaborated with the enemy

Divisione binaria two-regiment. The term indicates a structure whereby a divisional artillery acted as regimental batteries linked to the fighting infantry

Fasces lictoris the Roman rods and shield symbol that represented fascist authority

Fuoriuscito (plural fuoriusciti) political exiles of the fascist regime

Giardinetta Italian type of station wagon

Giovani italiane young fascist women between fourteen and seventeen belonging to the ranks of fascist youth organizations

Glasnost' openness. The term is used to describe Mikhail Gorbachev's policy promoting transparency in government activities in the Soviet Union in the 1980s

Izba Russian peasant hut

Kolkhoz collective farm

Kulak wealthy peasant

Linea pezzi the cannon shooting line

Makorka cheap tobacco used in Soviet times

Mani pulite clean hands. The term is used to describe Italy's corruption scandals of the 1990s

NKVD Ministry of Internal Affairs of the Soviet Union

Onor Caduti Commissariat Honoring the Fallen of War

Opera Vigilanza Repressione Antifascismo, OVRA Organization for Vigilance and Repression of Anti-Fascism

Osservazione e Collegamento, O.C. observation and communication. The term is used to indicate a patrol of artillerymen with special communication tasks

Partito Comunista Italiano, PCI Italian Communist Party

Podesta' head of the municipal administration during Fascism

Presenza alle Bandiere present to the flag. This phrase indicated an economic arrangement whereby the families of soldiers missing in action received a pension for a period of twelve months

Prikaz (plural prikazy) decree

Pshennaia kasha millet porridge

RAI UNO and RAI TRE Channel One and Three of the Italian Public Television

Regio Esercito Royal Army. The term is used to indicate the Italian Army from 1861 to 1946

Spetsgospital' special military hospital

Superinvalidita' the highest rank of disability in Italy

Tvorog cottage cheese

Unione Nazionale Italiana Reduci di Russia, or UNIRR Italian National Union of Veterans of Russia

Volkssturm the citizen army of young teenagers and old men mobilized in the German Army in the Fall of 1944

SELECTED FURTHER READINGS

Trauma, Memory, and Forgetting in Witness Accounts

Caruth, Cathy. *Trauma: Explorations in Memory*. Baltimore, MD: Johns Hopkins University Press, 1995.

Herman, Judith. *Trauma and Recovery: The Aftermath of Violence—from Domestic Abuse to Political Terror*. New York: Basic Books, 1992.

Hynes, Samuel. *The Soldiers' Tale. Bearing Witness to Modern War*. New York: Penguin Books, 1998.

LaCapra, Dominick. *Writing History, Writing Trauma*. Baltimore, MD: John Hopkins University Press, 2001.

Langer, Lawrence. *Holocaust Testimonies: The Ruins of Memory*. New Haven, CT: Yale University Press, 1991.

Wienand, Christiane. *Returning Memories: Former Prisoners of War in Divided and Reunited Germany*. Rochester, NY: Camden House, 2015.

Wieviorka, Annette. *The Era of the Witness*, trans. Jared Stark. Ithaca, NY: Cornell University Press, 2006.

Soviet Internment of Foreign Prisoners

Hilger, Andreas. "Re-Educating the German Prisoners of War: Aims, Methods, Results and Memory in East and West Germany." In *Prisoners of War, Prisoners of Peace: Captivity, Homecoming and Memory in World War II*, ed. Bob Moore and Barbara Hately-Broad, 61–75. Oxford: Berg, 2005.

Muminov, Sherzod. *Eleven Winters of Discontent: The Siberian Internment and the Making of a New Japan*. Cambridge, MA: Harvard University Press, 2022.

Zolotarev, Vladimir Antonovich and Aleksandr Sergeevich Emelin. eds. *Russkii arkhiv: Velikaia Otechestvennaia: Inostrannye voennoplennye Vtoroi mirovoi voiny v SSSR*, T.24 (13). Moscow: Terra, 1996.

Italian Soldiers in the Soviet Union

Antonelli, Quinto. ed. *"La propaganda e' l'unica nostra cultura"*. *Scritture autobiografiche dal fronte sovietico (1941–1943)*. Trento: Fondazione Museo Storico Trentino, 2016.

Giusti, Maria Teresa. *Stalin's Italian Prisoners of War*. New York: CEU Press, 2021.

Revelli, Nuto. *La Strada del Davai*. Einaudi: Torino, 1966.

Revelli, Nuto. *Mai Tardi. Diario di un Alpino in Russia*. Einaudi: Torino, 1967.

Rossi, Marina. "Opisanie vraga v dnevnikakh i svidetel'stvakh ital'ianskikh soldat, Ch.S.I.R i ARMIR 1941—1946." In *Tragediia plena*, ed. Arkadii Anisimovich Kuprennikov, 103–9. Krasnogorsk: Memorial'nyi Muzei Nemetskikh Antifashistov, 1996.

Sapori, Julien. *Marcher ou mourir: Les troupes italiennes on Russie 1941–1943*. Tours: Edition Sutton, 2018.

Scotoni, Giorgio. *L'Armata Rossa e la disfatta italiana (1942–1943)*. Trento: Panorama, 2007.

Scotoni, Giorgio. "Memoirs of the Russian Campaign and the New Semantics of the Italian Soldier," *Nauchnye Vedomosti. Seriia istoriia. Politiologiia* 1 (2017), 158–64.

Index